GLOSSARY

Institutions, policies
and enlargement
of the European Union

This booklet is published in all the official EU languages of the European Union: Danish, Dutch, English, Finnish, French, German, Greek, Italian, Portuguese, Spanish and Swedish.

European Commission
Directorate-General for Education and Culture
Publications Unit, rue de la Loi/Wetstraat 200, B-1049 Brussels

A great deal of additional information on the European Union is available on the Internet.
It can be accessed through the Europa server (http://europa.eu.int).

Cataloguing data can be found at the end of this publication.

Luxembourg: Office for Official Publications of the European Communities, 2000

ISBN 92-828-8282-9

Printed in Belgium

PRINTED ON WHITE CHLORINE-FREE PAPER

Foreword

This publication is an update of the previous edition of 'Glossary: *The reform of the European Union in 150 definitions*' that was produced in 1997.

As indicated by its original title, this glossary was produced in order to help people to gain a better understanding of the challenges facing the European Union at the time of the Intergovernmental Conference that opened in 1996. It was subsequently expanded to cover the fundamentals of European integration, the operation of the institutions, the policies of the Community and the contributions of the Amsterdam Treaty.

The inclusion of the essential aspects of the enlargement process and of Agenda 2000 and, in the future, the results of the Intergovernmental Conference of 2000, confirms the glossary's vocation of following European current affairs and explaining them to the public. An update of the definitions contained in this publication is available on the SCADPlus site, which can be accessed on the Europa server at the following address: http://europa.eu.int/scadplus/.

This document does not claim to be exhaustive in its definitions or information. It is an information tool for which the European Commission cannot be held responsible.

Abstention, constructive (positive abstention)

Constructive abstention is the idea of allowing a Member State to abstain on a vote in Council under the common foreign and security policy, without blocking a unanimous decision.

This option was introduced by the Treaty of Amsterdam in the new Article 23 of the EU Treaty. If constructive abstention is accompanied by a formal declaration, the Member State in question is not obliged to apply the decision but must accept that it commits the European Union. The Member State must then refrain from any action that might conflict with Union action based on that decision.

Accession criteria (Copenhagen criteria)

In June 1993, the Copenhagen European Council recognised the right of the countries of central and eastern Europe to join the European Union when they have fulfilled three criteria:

— political: stable institutions guaranteeing democracy, the rule of law, human rights and respect for minorities;
— economic: a functioning market economy;
— incorporation of the Community *acquis*: adherence to the various political, economic and monetary aims of the European Union.

These accession criteria were confirmed in December 1995 by the Madrid European Council, which also stressed the importance of adapting the applicant countries' administrative structures to create the conditions for a gradual, harmonious integration.

However, the Union reserves the right to decide when it will be ready to accept new members.

Accession negotiations

In 1995, it was decided to start negotiations with Cyprus. Although the applications of the 10 countries of central and eastern Europe were given a favourable reception at the Luxembourg European Council (December 1997), it was nonetheless decided to proceed in two phases. On 30 March 1998, negotiations began with the six 'first wave' countries (Cyprus, the Czech Republic, Estonia, Hungary, Poland, and Slovenia). The five other countries of central and eastern Europe (Bulgaria, Latvia, Lithuania, Romania and Slovakia), the 'second wave', will be able to join the first wave if it is felt that their reforms are progressing rapidly enough. The political and economic reforms and the state of incorporation of Community legislation are regularly monitored.

The evaluation of each applicant country's legislation will last until at least June 1999; a work programme can then be set up and negotiating positions defined. Thereafter, the negotiations proper with the first wave countries will begin, in the form of bilateral intergovernmental conferences (European Union/applicant country), which will bring the ministers together every six months and the ambassadors every month. The negotiations with the second wave countries will begin when the reforms they have undertaken are deemed sufficient.

Accession partnership

Concluded by the Council with each of the applicant countries (except Cyprus) in 1998, the accession partnerships coordinate the aid provided by the European Community to each country in central and eastern Europe and set priorities for each sector in adapting to Community legislation. The applicants' adherence to these priorities determines the Community's financial assistance.

Each country then draws up a detailed programme for the adoption of the Community *acquis* so as to organise the implementation of these priorities, committing itself to a timetable and indicating the human and financial resources needed to achieve it. This programme is adjusted as it goes along by the Commission and the country concerned. Economic priorities are also jointly established.

There are three financial instruments that will help support the reforms in the countries of central and eastern Europe under the accession partnerships from the year 2000:

— a pre-accession agricultural aid fund;
— a pre-accession structural aid fund;
— the Phare programme.

Agenda 2000

Agenda 2000 is an action programme adopted by the Commission on 15 July 1997 as an official response to requests by the Madrid European Council in December 1995 that it present a general document on enlargement and the reform of the common policies and a communication on the Union's future financial framework after 31 December 1999. Agenda 2000 tackles all the questions facing the Union at the beginning of the 21st century. Attached to it are the Commission's opinions on the countries that have applied for Union membership.

Agenda 2000 is in three parts:

— the first addresses the question of the European Union's internal operation, particularly the reform of the common agricultural policy and of the policy of economic and social cohesion. It also contains recommendations on how to face the challenge of enlargement in the best possible conditions and proposes putting in place a new financial framework for the period 2000–06;
— the second proposes a reinforced pre-accession strategy, incorporating two new elements: the partnership for accession and extended participation of the applicant countries in Community programmes and the mechanisms for applying the Community *acquis*;
— the third consists of a study on the impact of the effects of enlargement on European Union policies.

These priorities were fleshed out in some 20 legislative proposals put forward by the European Commission in 1998. The Berlin European Council reached an overall political agreement on the legislative package in 1999 with the result that the measures were adopted the same year. They cover four closely linked areas for the period 2000–06:

— reform of the common agricultural policy;
— reform of the structural policy;
— pre-accession instruments;
— financial framework.

Animal welfare

The question of animal welfare was first addressed in a declaration attached to the Treaty establishing the European Community on the occasion of the Intergovernmental Conference on political union (1991–92). The institutions have since then been required to take animal welfare into account when drafting and implementing Community legislation in the fields of the common agricultural policy, transport, the internal market and research.

A protocol laying down the obligations of the Community institutions and the Member States relating to animals was annexed to the EC Treaty by the Treaty of Amsterdam.

Applicant countries

Europe's economic and political stability is a magnet for many European countries, which have the right to apply to become members of the European Union (Article 49 of the EU Treaty, formerly Article O).

The countries that have applied are:

— Turkey: application received on 14 April 1987;
— Cyprus: 3 July 1990;
— Malta: 16 July 1990;
— Hungary: 31 March 1994;
— Poland: 5 April 1994;
— Romania: 22 June 1995;
— Slovakia: 27 June 1995;
— Latvia: 13 October 1995;
— Estonia: 24 November 1995;
— Lithuania: 8 December 1995;
— Bulgaria: 14 December 1995;
— Czech Republic: 17 January 1996;
— Slovenia: 10 June 1996.

In December 1997, the Luxembourg European Council decided to open negotiations in 1998 with six countries: Cyprus, the Czech Republic, Estonia, Hungary, Poland, and Slovenia. These six countries form the first wave of applicant countries. A second wave will be made up of Bulgaria, Latvia, Lithuania, Romania and Slovakia. Opening negotiations with these applicants will depend on their political and economic progress.

After two years, during which its application was put on ice (1996 to 1998), Malta has indicated that it intends to return to the negotiating table. A special report by the Commission on the progress made by Malta is due out soon. This will allow a decision to be taken on whether Malta can be included in the first or second wave of applicant countries. As far as Turkey is concerned, the Luxembourg European Council concluded that the political and economic conditions allowing accession negotiations to be envisaged were not yet satisfied, and that the European strategy to prepare Turkey for accession should be continued.

A European Conference brings the first- and second-wave applicant countries together every year.

For the record it should be remembered that Switzerland, Liechtenstein and Norway also all applied for membership of the European Union at various times. However, Norway twice rejected accession following referenda in 1972 and 1994, while the applications by Switzerland and Liechtenstein were shelved after Switzerland decided by a referendum in 1992 not to join the European Economic Area.

Architecture of Europe

This refers to the various organisations, institutions, treaties and traditional relations making up the European area within which members work together on problems of shared interest.

An essential part of this architecture was established by the Treaty on European Union, which formed three pillars: the European Community (first pillar), the common foreign and security policy (second pillar) and cooperation in the fields of justice and home affairs (third pillar). Matters falling within the second and third pillars are handled by the Community institutions (the European Council, the Council, the Commission, the European Parliament, etc.), but intergovernmental procedures apply.

Area of freedom, security and justice

The progress made since 1993 as a result of cooperation in the fields of justice and home affairs led to more ambitious objectives being enshrined in the Treaty of Amsterdam. It was decided to establish an area of freedom, security and justice, the aim being to ensure genuine freedom of movement for individuals on the territory of the European Union and more effective action against organised crime and fraud.

Matters relating to justice and home affairs used to be dealt with solely under the intergovernmental rules laid down in Title VI of the EU Treaty (the third pillar). With the entry into force of the Treaty of Amsterdam, these fields have been divided up between the first and third pillars.

Under the first pillar, which is governed by the Community method, a new Title IV has been added to the EC Treaty ('Visas, asylum, immigration and other policies related to free movement of persons'). Meanwhile the new Title VI of the EU Treaty now covers fewer fields, but its objectives are spelled out more clearly, namely to establish close cooperation between police services, customs and judicial authorities.

The third pillar provisions still include a 'bridge' allowing Member States to transfer areas of competence from Title VI to Title IV. The transfer procedure is very complex and has never been applied, but its existence suggests that in time all areas concerning justice and home affairs may be brought within the Community framework.

If some Member States wish to advance more quickly in certain fields and establish closer cooperation, they may do so within the European Union as specified in the new Article 40 of Title VI, without creating a separate legal system as happened with Schengen.

Article 36 Committee (EU Treaty, Title VI)

A Coordinating Committee consisting of senior officials was set up under Article 36 (former Article K.4) of the EU Treaty to prepare the ground for Council deliberations on police cooperation and judicial cooperation in civil matters. In practice the committee had already been in existence since the Rhodes European Council in December 1988.

Article 48, EU Treaty

Article 48 (former Article N) of the EU Treaty is the legal base which enables a conference of representatives of the Member States' governments (an IGC) to be convened for the purpose of amending the treaties. It stipulates that any Member State, or the Commission, may submit to the Council proposals for such amendments. If the Council, after consulting Parliament and the Commission, delivers an opinion in favour of calling a conference, it is convened by the President of the Council. Any subsequent amendments enter into force after being ratified by all the Member States in accordance with their respective constitutional requirements.

Article 49, EU Treaty

Accession of new Member States to the European Union is provided for in Article 49 (former Article O) of the EU Treaty. The Council must agree unanimously to open negotiations, after consulting the Commission and receiving the assent of the European Parliament. The conditions of admission, any transition periods and adjustments to the treaties on which the Union is founded must be the subject of an agreement between the applicant country and the Member State. To enter into force, the agreement requires ratification by all the contracting States in accordance with their respective constitutional requirements.

Article 308, EC Treaty

Article 308 of the EC Treaty (former Article 235) reflects the realisation by those who drafted the Treaty of Rome that the powers specifically allocated to the Community (executive powers) might not be adequate for the purpose of attaining the objectives expressly set by the treaties themselves (competence *ratione materiae*). This article can be used to bridge that gap, since it lays down that 'If action by the Community should prove necessary to attain ... one of the objectives of the Community and this Treaty has not provided the necessary powers, the Council shall, acting unanimously on a proposal from the Commission and after consulting the European Parliament, take the appropriate measures.'

Assent procedure

The assent procedure, whereby the Council must obtain Parliament's assent (absolute majority of its members) before certain important decisions can be taken, was introduced by the Single European Act. Parliament may accept or reject a proposal but cannot amend it.

The assent procedure mainly concerns the accession of new Member States and certain international agreements. It is also required for citizenship, the specific tasks of the European Central Bank, amendments to the Statute of the ESCB and of the ECB, the Structural and Cohesion Funds and the uniform procedure for elections to the European Parliament.

Following the entry into force of the Treaty of Amsterdam, Parliament's assent is also required in the event of sanctions being imposed on a Member State for a serious and persistent breach of fundamental rights under the new Article 7 of the EU Treaty.

Audiovisual

The audiovisual sector must respect various, sometimes contradictory principles such as competition rules (especially regarding State aid), the rules on intellectual property and the principles of public service. For these reasons, the European Community is having difficulties pursuing a genuine audiovisual policy.

Furthermore, the European audiovisual market is also facing the following problems:

— the language barriers preventing free movement of programmes;
— an unwieldy decision-making process which generally requires unanimity;
— the need to make considerable investment to anticipate technological developments, which requires international alliances and/or mergers.

The development of digital television and multimedia, and the explosion of demand for programmes to support the growth in the number of channels are all challenges for the European Community and its businesses in a sector that is constantly growing and creating new jobs.

Despite the difficulties mentioned above, the Community's activity in the audiovisual field has developed in two directions; industrial and legal.

— As far as developments in the industry are concerned, a directive was adopted in 1986 to ensure the standardisation of the systems used in the Member States to broadcast programmes by satellite and by cable. In 1989, objectives were defined for the development of high-definition television and then, in 1991, a single standard for broadcasting services and a financial support for a programme of cooperation between the businesses concerned was put in place. A subsidy programme intended to promote the 16:9 format was adopted in 1993.

— On the legal front, the Television without Frontiers Directive, adopted in 1989 and amended in 1997, provided a harmonised framework for the broadcasting of television programmes and facilitating their free movement. It established bases to support the production and distribution of European audiovisual programmes, introduced common rules on advertising, sponsorship, protection of minors and the right of reply, and introduced the requirement for TV channels to reserve, whenever possible, more than half of their transmission time for European works.

Furthermore, since 1991 the MEDIA programme (measures to promote the development of the audiovisual industry) has been supporting training schemes for professionals in the European audiovisual industry and promoting the development and distribution of European audiovisual works. MEDIA II (1996–2000) has a budget of EUR 310 million.

The Treaty of Amsterdam has added a protocol on the public broadcasting system in the Member States to the EC Treaty. The role of the Member States as regards public channels is made clear: they may continue to finance public service broadcasting as long as the broadcasting organisation fulfils a public service remit and its funding does not unfairly affect either trade or competition in the sector.

B

Budget

All the Union's revenue and expenditure is entered in the Community budget on the basis of the annual forecasts. The operational expenditure involved in implementing Titles V and VI of the EU Treaty may, however, constitute an exception to this rule by being charged to the Member States. In 1998 the Community budget totalled EUR 91 billion in commitment appropriations.

The Community budget is based on several principles, including:

— unity (all the revenue and expenditure is brought together in a single document);
— annuality (budget operations relate to a given budget year);
— equilibrium (expenditure must not exceed revenue).

The Commission is responsible for submitting a preliminary draft budget to the Council, which shares budgetary authority with the European Parliament. The nature of the expenditure determines which of the two institutions has the final say, depending on whether the expenditure is compulsory or not. However, quite apart from the classification of expenditure and the ensuing power-sharing, it should be remembered that it is the European Parliament that finally adopts or rejects the budget in its entirety.

Since 1993, the budget has been the subject of an interinstitutional agreement between Parliament, the Council and the Commission on budgetary discipline and improving the budgetary procedure. In 1998, the Commission presented a plan to renew the 1993 interinstitutional agreement in the light of experience gained in implementing it and to consolidate all the joint declarations and interinstitutional agreements on the budget concluded since 1982.

As part of the reforms proposed by the Commission in July 1997 in 'Agenda 2000', a new financial perspective will be adopted by the Member States to define the growth of the budget between 2000 and 2006.

C

Citizenship of the European Union

Citizenship of the Union is dependent on holding the nationality of one of the Member States. In other words, anyone who is a national of a Member State is considered to be a citizen of the Union. In addition to the rights and duties laid down in the Treaty establishing the European Community, Union citizenship confers four special rights:

— freedom to move and take up residence anywhere in the Union;
— the right to vote and stand in local government and European Parliament elections in the country of residence;
— diplomatic and consular protection from the authorities of any Member State where the country of which a person is a national is not represented in a non-Union country;
— the right of petition and appeal to the European Ombudsman.

The introduction of the notion of Union citizenship does not, of course, replace national citizenship: it is in addition to it. This gives the ordinary citizen a deeper and more tangible sense of belonging to the Union.

Civil protection, energy and tourism

Civil protection, energy and tourism are the subject of a declaration attached to the Treaty establishing the European Community.

The European Union has adopted a number of measures in these three areas on the basis of Article 308 (former Article 235), in the absence of any specific legal bases. In future the introduction of appropriate provisions into the Treaty could ensure the continuity and consistency of Community action, making it more easily comprehensible. Each of the three sectors has special features, however, which must not be ignored.

— The only area for which the European Union already has specific legal instruments, European energy policy, is still scattered throughout the ECSC and Euratom Treaties, on the one hand, and the general provisions of the Treaty establishing the European Community on the other.
— Measures on tourism have hitherto been carried out under the umbrella of other Union policies (environment, free movement of persons, training, etc.).
— Several resolutions have been adopted in the field of civil protection as a result of cooperation between Member States, despite the lack of an appropriate legal basis.

Clarity of the treaties (simplification of the treaties)

The Intergovernmental Conference (IGC) brought into sharp relief the question of the clarity of the treaties because of the nature of the Community legal structure, which is the result of a succession of amendments to the treaties. The need to simplify the treaty to make it more comprehensible for the ordinary citizen has been discussed.

The Treaty on European Union added a new structure amending and supplementing the existing ones and leaving a question mark hanging over certain provisions of the earlier treaties which it neither took over nor formally repealed.

The Commission does not want the difficulty of reading and understanding the founding texts of the Union to create a gulf between the Union and the public and has accordingly proposed that they be edited and consolidated.

In a joint declaration attached to the Treaty of Amsterdam, it was decided that work on consolidating all the treaties (including the Treaty on European Union) should be continued as speedily as possible so as to incorporate the amendments to previous treaties made by the Treaty of Amsterdam. The main object of the exercise is to produce legal texts that are clear and comprehensible to everyone. The results will have no legal value.

At the same time the articles of the treaties have been renumbered to make consultation easier.

Classification of expenditure

This refers to the distinction made between Union expenditure of which the underlying principle and the amount are legally determined by the treaties, secondary legislation, conventions, international treaties or private contracts ('compulsory' expenditure) and expenditure for which the budgetary authority is free to decide the amount as it sees fit ('non-compulsory' expenditure). The question of whether expenditure is to be considered compulsory or non-compulsory generates friction between the two arms of the budgetary authority — the Council and the European Parliament — as Parliament has the final say in determining the amount of expenditure only where it is non-compulsory. As agricultural expenditure is considered compulsory, the result is that more than 45 % of the Community budget is outside Parliament's control.

Closer cooperation

Closer cooperation is an idea written into the EU Treaty (Title VII) and the EC Treaty (Article 11) by the Treaty of Amsterdam. The aim of such cooperation is to enable a limited number of Member States that are willing and able to advance further, to deepen European integration within the single institutional framework of the Union.

Closer cooperation must meet a number of conditions. In particular it must:

— cover an area which does not fall within the exclusive competence of the Community;
— be aimed at furthering the objectives of the Union;
— respect the principles of the treaties;
— be used only as a last resort;
— involve a majority of Member States.

Closer cooperation under the EC Treaty is authorised by the Council, acting by a qualified majority on a proposal from the Commission and after consulting the European Parliament.

The object of closer cooperation under the EU Treaty is to develop the area of freedom, security and justice more swiftly. At the request of the Member States concerned, it is authorised by the Council, acting by a qualified majority after obtaining the Commission's opinion and after submitting the request to the European Parliament.

Co-decision procedure

The co-decision procedure (Article 251 of the EC Treaty, formerly Article 189b) was introduced by the Treaty of Maastricht. It gives the European Parliament the power to adopt instruments jointly with the Council. In practice, it has strengthened Parliament's legislative powers in the following fields: the free movement of workers, right of establishment, services, the internal market, education (incentive measures), health (incentive measures), consumer policy, trans-European networks (guidelines), environment (general action programme), culture (incentive measures) and research (framework programme).

In its 1996 report on the scope of the co-decision procedure, the Commission proposed that the procedure be extended to all Community legislative activity.

The Treaty of Amsterdam has simplified the co-decision procedure, making it quicker, more effective and more transparent. And it has been extended to new areas such as social exclusion, public health and the fight against fraud affecting the European Community's financial interests.

Collective defence

Collective defence is the term used to describe Europe's participation in defence under the treaties of Brussels (Article V) and Washington (Article 5), which stipulate that the signatory States are required, in the event of aggression, to provide assistance for the restoration of security.

Since 1949 the organisation set up by the Washington Treaty (NATO) has been the principal guarantor of security in western Europe, whereas Western European Union (WEU) has simply been ticking over for nearly 30 years. It should be noted, however, that WEU is the only strictly European organisation to have established an automatic collective defence obligation. With the development of a European defence identity, WEU today is destined to play a bigger role.

Comitology

Under the Treaty establishing the European Community, it is for the Commission to implement legislation at Community level (Article 202 of the EC Treaty, ex-Article 145). In practice, each legislative instrument specifies the scope of the implementing powers granted to the Commission and how the Commission is to use them. Frequently, the instrument will also make provision for the Commission to be assisted by a committee in accordance with a procedure known as 'comitology'.

The committees which are forums for discussion, consist of representatives from Member States and are chaired by the Commission. They enable the Commission to establish a dialogue with national administrations before adopting implementing measures. The Commission ensures that they reflect as far as possible the situation in each country in question.

Procedures which govern relations between the Commission and the committees are based on models set out in a Council Decision ('comitology' Decision). The first 'comitology' Decision dates back to 13 July 1987. In order to take into account the changes in the Treaty — and, in particular, Parliament's new position under the co-decision procedure — but also to reply to criticisms that the Community system is too complex and too opaque, the 1987 Decision has been replaced by the Council Decision of 28 June 1999.

The new Decision ensures that Parliament can keep an eye on the implementation of legislative instruments adopted under the co-decision procedure. In cases where legislation comes under this procedure, Parliament can express its disapproval of measures proposed by the Commission or, where appropriate, by the Council, which go beyond the implementing powers provided for in the legislation, in Parliament's opinion.

The Decision clarifies the criteria to be applied to the choice of committee and simplifies the operational procedures. Committees base their opinions on the draft implementing measures prepared by the Commission. The committees can be divided into the following categories.

— Advisory committees: they give their opinions to the Commission which must take the utmost account of them. This straightforward procedure is generally used when the matters under discussion are not very sensitive politically.

— Management committees: where the measures adopted by the Commission are not consistent with the committee's opinion (delivered by qualified majority), the Commission must communicate them to the Council which, acting by a qualified majority, can take a different decision. This procedure is used in particular for measures relating to the management of the common agricultural policy, fisheries, and the main Community programmes.

— Regulatory committees: the Commission can only adopt implementing measures if it obtains the approval by qualified majority of the Member States meeting within the committee. In the absence of such support, the proposed measure is referred back to the Council which takes a decision by qualified majority. However, if the Council does not take a decision, the Commission finally adopts the implementing measure provided that the Council does not object by a qualified majority. This procedure is used for measures relating to protection of the health or safety of persons, animals and plants and measures amending non-essential provisions of the basic legislative instruments.

It also provides the criteria which, depending on the matter under discussion, will guide the legislative authority in its choice of committee procedure for the item of legislation; this is meant to facilitate the adoption of the legislation under the co-decision procedure.

Lastly, several innovations in the new 'comitology' Decision enhance the transparency of the committee system to the benefit of Parliament and the general public: committee documents will be more readily accessible to the citizen (the arrangements are the same as those applying to Commission documents). Committee documents will also be registered in a public register which will be available from 2001 onwards. The ultimate aim is, with the computerisation of decision-making procedures, to publish the full texts of non-confidential documents transmitted to Parliament on the Internet. From 2000 onwards, the Commission will publish an annual report giving a summary of committee activities during the previous year.

Committee of the Regions

Set up by the Maastricht Treaty, the Committee of the Regions consists of 222 representatives of local and regional authorities appointed by the Council for four years on the basis of proposals from the Member States. It is consulted by the Council or the Commission in areas affecting regional interests, such as education, youth, culture, health and social and economic cohesion.

Following the entry into force of the Treaty of Amsterdam, the Committee has to be consulted on an even wider range of fields — the environment, the Social Fund, vocational training, cross-border cooperation and transport.

It may also issue opinions on its own initiative and may be consulted by the European Parliament.

Committees and working parties

The committees, whose task it is to assist the Community institutions, are involved at all stages of the legislative process. The Commission regularly consults committees of experts before drawing up a new proposal for legislation. These committees, which are made up of representatives of the milieux involved, private sector or national government experts, ensure that the Commission remains open to the concerns of those who will be affected by the legislation. There are about 60 advisory committees covering all sectors, though about half of them deal with agricultural issues.

In the European Parliament, various permanent committees organise the work of the MEPs.

The Council is also assisted by committees and working parties which prepare its decisions. The existence of certain committees is provided for in the treaties (Article 36 Committee for justice and home affairs, for example), and others are ad hoc committees such as the Cultural Affairs Committee, which evaluates proposals on cultural cooperation, prepares the Council discussions and follows up action taken. These committees are made up of representatives of the Member States plus one member of the Commission. In parallel, various working parties do the preparatory work for Coreper. While some of them are set up on a temporary basis to deal with a particular dossier, about 100 groups cover a given sector and meet regularly.

When a legislative text has been adopted, it lays down the general principles to be respected. More precise implementing measures may be necessary to apply these principles. In this case, the text provides that a committee is to be set up within the Commission in order to take the appropriate decisions. These committees are made up of experts nominated by the Member States and chaired by the Commission, and are generally governed by rules established by the 1987 Council decision known as the 'Comitology Decision'. There are about 300 of them, in the fields of industry, social affairs, agriculture, the environment, the internal market, research and development, consumer protection and food safety.

Common agricultural policy (CAP)

The common agricultural policy is a matter reserved exclusively for the Community. Under Article 33 of the EC Treaty (former Article 39), its aims are to ensure reasonable prices for Europe's consumers and fair incomes for farmers, in particular by establishing common agricultural market organisations and by applying the principles of single prices, financial solidarity and Community preference.

The CAP is one of the most important Union policies (agricultural expenditure accounts for some 45 % of the Community budget). Policy is decided by qualified majority vote in the Council after consultation of the European Parliament.

At the outset the CAP enabled the Community to become self-sufficient in a very short time. However, it came to be increasingly costly because European prices were too high by comparison with world market prices. A series of reforms in 1992 corrected the situation by cutting guaranteed farm prices, with compensatory premiums for inputs, and by introducing a series of 'flanking measures'.

With a view to enlargement a new reform package was adopted in 1999 for the period 2000–06. Under the approach proposed by the Commission in Agenda 2000 in July 1997, it reinforces the changes made in 1992 and puts the emphasis on food safety, environmental objectives and sustainable agriculture. Moreover, it endeavours to increase the competitiveness of Community agricultural products, simplify agricultural legislation and how it is implemented and strengthen the Union's position at the World Trade Organisation negotiations (Millennium Round), and lastly stabilise agriculture expenditure.

In this spirit, changes have already been made in the common organisation of the market in wine, arable crops, beef and veal and milk. The proposed reduction in intervention prices has been off-set by an increase in aid to farmers and accompanied by a genuine integrated rural development policy.

Common commercial policy

The Community has exclusive responsibility for the common commercial policy (Article 133 of the EC Treaty, formerly Article 113). Under the policy a customs union has been established between the Member States of the Community, with uniform principles governing changes in tariff rates, the conclusion of tariff and trade agreements with non-member countries, import and export policy, etc., decisions are taken by qualified majority in the Council.

The Treaty of Amsterdam amended Article 113 to allow the Council, acting by unanimous vote, to extend the scope of the common commercial policy to international negotiations and agreements on services and intellectual property.

Common defence policy

The European Union's common foreign and security policy includes the eventual framing of a common defence policy which might in time lead to a common defence. On defence matters, the European Union requests Western European Union (WEU) to elaborate and implement decisions and actions which have defence implications (Article 17 of the EU Treaty, formerly Article J.4).

The common defence policy is one element of a security policy in the broadest sense of the term. Its aim is to reduce the risks which threaten the common values and fundamental interests of the Union and its Member States, and to help preserve and strengthen peace in accordance with the United Nations Charter, the Helsinki Final Act, the Washington Treaty (NATO) and the amended Brussels Treaty (WEU).

An important innovation made by the Treaty of Amsterdam is the inclusion in the EU Treaty of a reference to the so-called Petersberg tasks (humanitarian and rescue operations, peacekeeping operations and the use of combat forces in crisis management).

Common foreign and security policy (CFSP)

The common foreign and security policy (CFSP) was established and is governed by Title V of the EU Treaty. It replaced European Political Cooperation (EPC) and provides for the eventual framing of a common defence policy which might in time lead to a common defence.

The objectives of this second pillar of the Union are set out in Article 11 (former Article J.1), and are to be attained through specific legal instruments (joint action, common position) which have to be adopted unanimously in the Council. With the entry into force of the Treaty of Amsterdam, the Union also has a new instrument at its disposal — the common strategy, which is referred to in the new Article 12.

Common position (CFSP)

The common position in the context of the common foreign and security policy is designed to make cooperation more systematic and improve its coordination. The Member States are required to comply with and uphold such positions which have been adopted unanimously at Council meetings.

Common strategy (CFSP)

The common strategy is a new instrument introduced under the common foreign and security policy by the Treaty of Amsterdam.

Under the new Article 13 of the EU Treaty, the European Council defines the principles and general guidelines for the CFSP and decides on common strategies to be implemented by the Union in fields where the Member States have important interests in common.

In concrete terms, a common strategy sets out the aims and length of time covered and the means to be made available by the Union and the Member States. Common strategies are implemented by the Council, in particular by adopting joint actions and common positions. The Council can recommend common strategies to the European Council.

Common transport policy

The aim of the common transport policy is to lay down common rules applicable to international transport to or from the territory of the Member States or passing across the territory of one or more of them

(Articles 70 to 80 of the EC Treaty). It is also concerned with laying down the conditions under which non-resident carriers may operate services within a Member State; and lastly, it covers measures to improve transport safety.

With the entry into force of the Treaty of Amsterdam, decisions are now taken under the co-decision procedure (Article 251 of the EC Treaty), after the Economic and Social Committee and the Committee of the Regions have been consulted. However, some special cases still remain:

— measures that are liable to have a major impact on living standards, employment and the operation of transport facilities are adopted by the Council acting unanimously, after consulting the European Parliament and the Economic and Social Committee;
— in the case of specific measures relating to sea and air transport, the Council decides what procedure to apply in each individual instance, acting by a qualified majority.

Communitisation

Communitisation means transferring a matter which, in the institutional framework of the Union, is dealt with using the intergovernmental method (second and third pillars) to the Community method (first pillar).

The Community method is based on the idea that the general interest of Union citizens is best defended when the Community institutions play their full role in the decision-making process, with due regard for the subsidiarity principle.

Following the entry into force of the Treaty of Amsterdam, questions relating to the free movement of persons, which used to come under cooperation on justice and home affairs (third pillar), have been 'communitised' and so will be dealt with under the Community method after a five-year transitional phase.

Community *acquis*

The Community *acquis* or Community patrimony is the body of common rights and obligations which bind all the Member States together within the European Union. It is constantly evolving and comprises:

— the content, principles and political objectives of the treaties;
— the legislation adopted in application of the treaties and the case law of the Court of Justice;
— the declarations and resolutions adopted by the Union;
— measures relating to the common foreign and security policy;
— measures relating to justice and home affairs;
— international agreements concluded by the Community and those concluded by the Member States between themselves in the field of the Union's activities.

Thus the Community *acquis* comprises not only Community law in the strict sense, but also all acts adopted under the second and third pillars of the European Union and, above all, the common objectives laid down in the treaties.

Applicant countries have to accept the Community *acquis* before they can join the European Union. Exemptions and derogations from the *acquis* are granted only in exceptional circumstances and are limited in scope. The Union has committed itself to maintaining the Community *acquis* in its entirety and developing it further. There is no question of going back on it.

In preparation for the accession of new Member States, the Commission is currently examining with the applicant countries how far their legislation conforms to the Community *acquis*.

Community and intergovernmental methods

The Community method is the expression used for the institutional operating mode set up in the first pillar of the European Union. It proceeds from an integration logic with due respect for the subsidiarity principle, and has the following salient features:

— Commission monopoly of the right of initiative;
— widespread use of qualified majority voting in the Council;
— an active role for the European Parliament;
— uniform interpretation of Community law by the Court of Justice.

It contrasts with the intergovernmental method of operation used in the second and third pillars, which proceeds from an intergovernmental logic of cooperation and has the following salient features:

— the Commission's right of initiative is shared with the Member States or confined to specific areas of activity;
— the Council generally acts unanimously;
— the European Parliament has a purely consultative role;
— the Court of Justice plays only a minor role.

Community 'bridge' (Title VI of the EU Treaty)

The Treaty of Maastricht introduced the possibility of bringing some areas covered by Title VI of the EU Treaty under the Community framework (qualified majority voting, as provided for in the former Article 100c). This procedure, known as the 'bridge', required unanimity in the Council and ratification by each Member State in accordance with its national constitutional requirements.

With the entry into force of the Treaty of Amsterdam, any areas falling under the new Article 29 in Title VI may be transferred to the new Title IV of the EC Treaty. As in the past, any decision to bring such matters within the Community framework will have to be taken by the Council unanimously and ratified by each Member State.

Community law

Strictly speaking, Community law consists of the founding treaties (primary legislation) and the provisions of instruments enacted by the Community institutions by virtue of them (secondary legislation).

In a broader sense, Community law encompasses all the rules of the Community legal order, including general principles of law, the case law of the Court of Justice, law flowing from the Community's external relations and supplementary law contained in conventions and similar agreements concluded between the Member States to give effect to treaty provisions.

All these rules of law form part of what is known as the Community *acquis*.

Community legal instruments

The term Community legal instruments refers to the instruments available to the Community institutions to carry out their tasks under the Treaty establishing the European Community with due respect for the subsidiarity principle. They are:

— regulations: these are binding in their entirety and directly applicable in all Member States;
— directives: these bind the Member States as to the results to be achieved; they have to be transposed

into the national legal framework and thus leave a margin for manoeuvre as to the form and means of implementation;

— decisions: these are fully binding on those to whom they are addressed;

— recommendations and opinions: these are non-binding, declaratory instruments.

Competition

The rules on competition are intended to ensure that a European economic area based on market forces can function effectively. The European Community's competition policy (Articles 81 to 89 of the EC Treaty, formerly 85 to 94) is based on five main principles:

— the prohibition of concerted practices, agreements and associations between undertakings which may affect trade between Member States and prevent, restrict or distort competition within the common market;

— the prohibition of abuse of a dominant position within the common market, insofar as it may affect trade between Member States;

— supervision of aid granted by the Member States, or through State resources in whatever form whatsoever, which threatens to distort competition by favouring certain undertakings or the production of certain goods;

— preventive supervision of mergers with a European dimension, by approving or prohibiting the envisaged alliances;

— liberalisation of certain sectors where public or private enterprises have hitherto evolved monopolistically, such as telecommunications, transport or energy.

The first two principles may, however, be subject to derogations, particularly when an agreement between undertakings improves the production or distribution of products or promotes technical progress. In the case of State aid schemes, social subsidies, or subsidies to promote culture and conservation of heritage, are also examples of possible exceptions to the strict application of competition rules.

The difficulty of pursuing an effective competition policy lies in the fact that the Community must continually juggle aims that are sometimes contradictory, since it has to ensure that:

— the quest for perfect competition on the internal market does not make European businesses less competitive on the world market;

— efforts to liberalise do not threaten the maintenance of public services meeting basic needs.

Competitiveness

The European Commission's 1994 White Paper on growth, competitiveness and employment contains guidelines for a policy of global competitiveness. The policy encompasses four objectives which have lost none of their topicality today:

— helping European firms to adapt to the new globalised and interdependent competitive situation;

— exploiting the competitive advantages associated with the gradual shift to a knowledge-based economy;

— promoting a sustainable development of industry;

— reducing the time-lag between the pace of change in supply and the corresponding adjustments in demand.

The new title on employment incorporated in the EC Treaty by the Treaty of Amsterdam takes account of the objectives set in the White Paper.

Composition of the Commission

The question of the composition of the Commission was the subject of much discussion at the Intergovernmental Conference that drafted the Treaty of Amsterdam, although no immediate decision was taken. The problem is to determine what is the optimum number of Commissioners needed to guarantee the legitimacy, collective responsibility and efficiency of an institution whose purpose is to represent the general interest and whose Members are completely independent.

The discussion about the composition of the Commission is closely linked to the question of collective responsibility, a term used to describe a particular feature of the Commission structure whereby positions adopted by the Commission reflect the views of the Commission as a whole, not those of individual members. With the prospect of future enlargements, there are fears that a large increase in the number of Commissioners will lead to nationalisation of the office at the expense of collective responsibility. Conversely, should the number be limited, the fear is that some nationalities will not be represented among the Commissioners.

A protocol on the institutions was annexed to the EU Treaty by the Treaty of Amsterdam. It states that when the Union is next enlarged, the Commission will comprise one Commissioner of each nationality, provided that the weighting of votes in the Council has been modified in a manner acceptable to all the Member States. One year before the membership of the European Union exceeds 20, a new intergovernmental conference will have to be convened to carry out a comprehensive review of the composition and functioning of the institutions. If the European Union is to operate properly with more than 20 members, its present procedures will have to be entirely reorganised.

Concentric circles

This concept involves a Europe structured out of subsets of States which have achieved different levels of integration. It is not confined just to the integration structure of the European Union, and the idea has been expanded upon by a number of prominent figures. Some of them talk of 'the circle of shared law' (the Union's Member States), the 'adjacent circle' (the countries outside the Union waiting to join it) and 'more select circles' for the purpose of greater cooperation (the currency circle, the defence circle and so on).

Conciliation Committee

Under the co-decision procedure between Council and Parliament, a Conciliation Committee may be set up as provided for in Article 251(4) (former Article 189b(4)) of the EU Treaty. It comprises the members of the Council or their representatives and an equal number of representatives of Parliament. Any disagreement between the two institutions on the outcome of a co-decision procedure is referred to the Committee with a view to reaching agreement on a text acceptable to both sides.

The draft of any joint text must then be adopted within six weeks by qualified majority in the Council and by an absolute majority of the Members of Parliament. Should one of the two institutions reject the proposal, it is deemed not to have been adopted.

Confirmation of the Commission

The Treaties of Maastricht and then Amsterdam have completely overhauled the procedure for appointing the Commission, introducing confirmation of the appointments. There are now two separate procedures, the first concerning the President and the second the entire Commission.

To begin with the governments of the Member States nominate the person they intend to appoint as President of the Commission by common accord, after consulting the European Parliament. Their nominee is then approved by the European Parliament (this part of the procedure is an innovation introduced by the Treaty of Amsterdam). After that the Member States nominate the other persons they intend to appoint as Members, in consultation with the nominee for President. The entire Commission is then subject to a vote of approval by the European Parliament and finally appointed by the governments of the Member States.

This procedure was first applied at the beginning of the 1995–99 legislative period. It has the twofold advantage of enhancing the Commission's legitimacy and the dialogue between the two institutions.

Consolidation of legislation — formal/official

Formal or official consolidation of legislation involves adopting a new legal instrument, published in the Official Journal (L series), which incorporates and repeals the instruments being consolidated (basic instrument + amending instrument(s)) without altering their substance. It can be:

— vertical: the new instrument incorporates the basic instrument and instruments amending it into a single instrument;
— horizontal: the new instrument incorporates several parallel basic instruments — and amendments thereto — relating to the same matter into a single instrument.

Consolidation of legislation — informal/declaratory

There is a special procedure for unofficial, purely declaratory consolidation of legislation and simplification of legal instruments. The incorporation of subsequent amendments into the body of a basic act does not entail the adoption of a new instrument. It is simply a clarification exercise conducted by the Commission. The resulting text, which has no formal legal effect, can, where appropriate, be published in the Official Journal (C series) without citations or recitals.

Consultation procedure

Under this procedure the Council must consult the European Parliament and take its views into account. However, it is not bound by Parliament's position but only by the obligation to consult it. The procedure applies in particular to the common agricultural policy.

Consumer protection

Consumer protection is dealt with in Article 153 of the EC Treaty (former Article 129a), which was inserted by the Treaty of Maastricht. It is intended to promote consumers' health, safety, economic and legal interests, and their right to information.

Article 153 explicitly refers to another legal basis for the attainment of its objectives, namely to Article 95 (former Article 100a), which requires the co-decision procedure for all measures involving closer alignment of Member States' legislation on completion of the single market where consumer protection is concerned. At the same time, it stipulates that specific action supporting and supplementing the policy pursued by the Member States is to be adopted under the co-decision procedure, after consultation of the Economic and Social Committee.

A Member State may keep or introduce stricter consumer protection measures than those laid down by the Community, as long as they are compatible with the Treaty and the Commission is notified of them.

Convention (EU Treaty, Title VI)

Cooperation on justice and home affairs (Title VI of the EU Treaty) was introduced by the Treaty of Maastricht in 1993. This made provision for various specific instruments, including conventions. Since the entry into force of the Treaty of Amsterdam, conventions may only be used for police and judicial cooperation in criminal matters and they are now governed by new rules.

Based on the new Article 34 of the EU Treaty, a convention is adopted by unanimous decision of the Council after consulting the European Parliament and then ratified by the Member States in accordance with their respective constitutional procedures. After being ratified by at least half the Member States, a convention enters into force in those States.

The Court of Justice now has jurisdiction to give preliminary rulings on their interpretation and to rule on any disputes regarding their application. However, its role is subject to approval by the Member States. Each of them must make a declaration stating that they accept the Court's jurisdiction and designating the national courts that may refer questions to it.

Convergence criteria

To ensure that the sustainable convergence required for the achievement of economic and monetary union (EMU) comes about, the Treaty sets five convergence criteria which must be met by each Member State before it can take part in the third stage of EMU. The Commission and the European Central Bank (ECB) draw up reports to check whether the criteria are being met. The criteria are:

— the ratio of government deficit to gross domestic product must not exceed 3 %;
— the ratio of government debt to gross domestic product must not exceed 60 %;
— there must be a sustainable degree of price stability and an average inflation rate, observed over a period of one year before the examination, which does not exceed by more than one and a half percentage points that of the three best performing Member States in terms of price stability;
— there must be a long-term nominal interest rate which does not exceed by more than two percentage points that of the three best performing Member States in terms of price stability;
— the normal fluctuation margins provided for by the exchange-rate mechanism on the European Monetary system must have been respected without severe tensions for at least the last two years before the examination.

The convergence criteria, then, are meant to ensure that economic development within EMU is balanced and does not give rise to any tensions between the Member States. It must also be remembered that the criteria relating to government deficit and government debt must continue to be met after the start of the third stage of EMU (1 January 1999). A stability pact with this end in view was adopted at the Amsterdam European Council in June 1997.

Cooperation procedure

The cooperation procedure (Article 252 of the EC Treaty, formerly Article 189c) was introduced by the Single European Act. It gave Parliament greater influence in the legislative process by allowing it two 'readings' of Commission proposals. After the EU Treaty came into force it applied to the following areas in particular: transport, non-discrimination, implementation of Article 101 (funds of the European Central Bank or the central banks of the Member States), the Social Fund, vocational training, trans-European networks, economic and social cohesion, research, environment, development cooperation, health and safety of workers (Article 138), the Social Policy Agreement, etc.

With the entry into force of the Treaty of Amsterdam, the scope of the cooperation procedure has been considerably reduced in favour of the co-decision procedure (Article 251 of the EC Treaty). The cooperation procedure now applies only to certain aspects of economic and monetary union.

Coordinated strategy for employment

The Treaty of Amsterdam introduces the concept of a coordinated strategy for employment which follows on from the integrated strategy for employment launched at the Essen European Council in December 1994.

At Essen the European Council asked the Member States to draw up multiannual programmes for employment (MAPs) and provide the Commission with reports on their implementation. These reports describe the main measures taken by the governments to apply their multiannual programmes over the last twelve months, assess the impact of these measures on employment — in certain cases — and announce major changes or new initiatives in this field.

The 'Essen strategy' was refined by the European Council in Madrid (December 1995) and Dublin (December 1996), on both occasions on the basis of a joint report by the Commission and the Council summarising the reports on the implementation of the MAPs. At Florence (June 1996) and Amsterdam (June 1997), the European Council received a more succinct interim joint report.

With the Treaty of Amsterdam, a new title on employment has been written into the EC Treaty, introducing the concepts of a coordinated strategy and guidelines for employment. In practical terms, there will be two main innovations:

— the Council draws up guidelines for employment each year that are compatible with the broad lines of economic policy; it does so acting by a qualified majority on a proposal from the Commission and after consulting the European Parliament, the Economic and Social Committee, the Committee of the Regions and the Employment Committee;
— the Council can also make recommendations to the Member States in the light of its annual review of their employment policies, acting by a qualified majority on a recommendation from the Commission.

The Amsterdam European Council decided that the relevant provisions of the new title on employment should be put into effect immediately and they have been applied since June 1997.

Coreper

Coreper, the French acronym by which the Permanent Representatives Committee is known, consists of the Member States' Permanent Representatives (Ambassadors) and is responsible, at a stage involving preliminary negotiations, for assisting the Council of the European Union in dealing with the items on its agenda (proposals and drafts of instruments put forward by the Commission). It occupies a pivotal position in the Community decision-making system, in which it is at one and the same time a forum for dialogue (among the Permanent Representatives and between them and their respective national capitals) and a body which exercises political control (by laying down guidelines for, and supervising, the work of the expert groups). It is in fact divided in two to enable it to deal with all the tasks it has to carry out:

— Coreper I, consisting of the Deputy Permanent Representatives, and
— Coreper II, consisting of the Permanent Representatives themselves.

The smooth running of the Council is dependent on the standard of the work done in Coreper.

COREU (CFSP)

COREU is an EU communication network between the Member States and the Commission for cooperation in the fields of foreign policy. It makes it easier for decisions to be taken swiftly in emergencies.

Council of the European Union

The Council of the Union (Council, sometimes referred to as the Council of Ministers) is the European Union's main decision-making institution. It consists of the ministers of the 15 Member States responsible for the matters on the agenda: foreign affairs, farming, industry, transport or whatever. Despite the existence of these different ministerial compositions depending on the matter in hand, the Council is nonetheless a single institution.

Each country in the Union in turn holds the chair for six months. Decisions are prepared by the Committee of Permanent Representatives of the Member States (Coreper), assisted by working parties of national government officials. The Council is assisted by its General Secretariat.

Following the entry into force of the Treaty of Amsterdam, the Secretary-General acts as High Representative for the common foreign and security policy. He is assisted by a Deputy Secretary-General appointed by unanimous decision of the Council, who is responsible for running the Council's General Secretariat.

Qualified majority voting in the Council now applies to most of the new provisions (incentive measures in employment and social policy, public health and fraud prevention) and for the adoption of the framework programme on research. Some observers feel that qualified majority voting should have been extended further to avoid the risk of stalemate that is always present when decisions are taken unanimously. Given the prospect of the enlargement of the Union, Belgium, France and Italy considered that extension of qualified majority voting was a matter of crucial importance and made a declaration to that effect which is attached to the Final Act of the Intergovernmental Conference. The debate will continue at a new intergovernmental conference that is due to be convened at least one year before the membership of the Union exceeds 20 in order to carry out a comprehensive review of the composition and functioning of the institutions.

Court of Auditors

The Court of Auditors is composed of 15 members appointed for six years by unanimous decision of the Council after consulting the European Parliament. It audits Union revenue and expenditure to make sure it is lawful and proper and ensures that financial management is sound. It was set up in 1977 and raised to full institution status by the EU Treaty.

Under the Treaty of Amsterdam, the Court of Auditors now also has the power to report any irregularities to the European Parliament and the Council, and its audit responsibilities have been extended to Community funds managed by outside bodies and by the European Investment Bank.

Court of Justice

The Court of Justice of the European Communities is made up of 15 judges assisted by nine advocates-general appointed for six years by agreement among the Member States. It has two principal functions: to check whether instruments of the European institutions and of governments are compatible with the treaties, and, at the request of a national court, to pronounce on the interpretation or the validity of provisions contained in Community law.

The Court is assisted by a Court of First Instance, set up in 1989, which has special responsibility for dealing with administrative disputes in the European institutions and disputes arising from the Community competition rules.

Culture

Culture was brought within the Community sphere by the EU Treaty. Article 151 of the EC Treaty (former Article 128) requires the Community to encourage cultural cooperation between Member States and, if necessary, supplement their action in:

— the dissemination of the culture and history of the European peoples;
— the conservation and safeguarding of cultural heritage of European significance;
— non-commercial cultural exchanges;
— artistic, literary and audiovisual creation;
— cooperation with third countries and the competent international organisations, in particular the Council of Europe.

Action in these areas is decided on unanimously by the Council according to the co-decision procedure, after consulting the Committee of the Regions. Recommendations may also be adopted by the Council, acting unanimously, on a Commission proposal.

Various programmes have been adopted since 1990, such as Kaleidoscope (support for European cultural events and artistic creation), Ariane (for books and reading) and Raphael (for the conservation and development of heritage). The European Community has also supported the Member States' initiative whereby they have designated a 'European City of Culture' each year since 1985. In order to ensure greater coherence for the initiatives carried out by the Community, the Commission would like to see a framework programme covering the period 2000–04 to be adopted, entitled 'Culture 2000'.

In parallel, other actions are being carried out under the Community's economic and social policies (support for artists, development of a European cultural industry).

D

Decision and framework decision (EU Treaty, Title VI)

With the entry into force of the Treaty of Amsterdam, these new instruments under Title VI of the EU Treaty (Police and judicial cooperation in criminal matters) have replaced joint action. More binding and more authoritative, they should serve to make action under the reorganised third pillar more effective.

Framework decisions are used to approximate (align) the laws and regulations of the Member States. Proposals are made on the initiative of the Commission or a Member State and they have to be adopted unanimously. They are binding on the Member States as to the result to be achieved but leave the choice of form and methods to the national authorities.

Decisions are used for any purpose other than approximating the laws and regulations of the Member States. They are binding and any measures required to implement them at Union level are adopted by the Council acting by a qualified majority.

Declaration (CFSP)

The Declaration is an instrument for which there is no provision in Title V of the Treaty on European Union but which was a feature of European political cooperation (EPC). It is not a mandatory instrument and is still frequently used under the common foreign and security policy (CFSP).

Deepening

Deepening refers to the integration dynamic present from the outset of the European venture. Through the customs union, the common market, and then the Euro zone, the European Communities have grown into what aspires to be an 'ever closer union' among the peoples of Europe (Article 1 of the EU Treaty). Deepening is a process parallel to, and often viewed as a necessary step prior to, enlargement.

In this spirit it has been decided to reform the main Community policies (common agricultural policy and structural policy) and the workings of the institutions to create a favourable context for new Member States to join the European Union.

Democratic deficit

The democratic deficit is a concept invoked principally in the argument that the European Union suffers from a lack of democracy and is becoming remote from the ordinary citizen because its method of operating is so complex. The view is that the Community institutional set-up is dominated by an institution combining legislative and government powers (the Council) and an institution that lacks democratic legitimacy (the Commission — even though its Members are appointed by the Member States, subject to a vote of approval by the European Parliament, and collectively accountable to Parliament).

The view that the Community suffers from a democratic deficit should diminish after the entry into force of the Treaty of Amsterdam, which provides for an extension of the European Parliament's powers and a regular supply of information to national parliaments. The Treaty also states that it 'marks a new stage in the process of creating an ever closer union among the peoples of Europe, in which decisions are taken as openly as possible and as closely as possible to the citizen'.

Differentiated integration (flexibility)

Differentiated integration means a process of integration in which the Member States opt to move forward at different speeds and/or towards different objectives, in contrast to the notion of a monolithic bloc of States pursuing identical objectives at a single speed.

With the entry into force of the Treaty of Amsterdam, the concept of differentiated integration has found practical expression in a number of general clauses dealing with closer cooperation that have been written into the EU and the EC treaties.

Double majority

Given the prospect of an enlarged European Union, proposals have been put together for maintaining the current balance between 'large' countries and 'small' countries in Council decision-making. Requiring a majority both of the Member States and of the population of the Union to be in favour before any decision can be taken in the Council would be a way of avoiding what some see as the over-representation of the smaller countries.

For instance, the qualified-majority threshold (currently about 70 %) could be maintained, but Member States voting in favour would have to represent three fifths of the total population. The thresholds for this double majority could vary depending on the subject.

The institutional question of how decisions will be taken in an enlarged Europe was not resolved at the 1996–97 Intergovernmental Conference. Under the Treaty of Amsterdam, a protocol on the institutions with the prospect of enlargement was annexed to the EU Treaty, linking the question of decision-making in the Council to the number of Commissioners. The protocol states that from the date of the next enlargement, the Commission will comprise one national of each Member State, provided that the weighting of the votes in the Council has been modified by then, either by re-weighting or by double majority. It also provides for a new intergovernmental conference to be convened at least one year before the Union's membership exceeds 20, in order to review the rules on the functioning of the Union institutions.

E

Economic and monetary union

Economic and monetary union (EMU) is the process whereby the economic and monetary policies of the Member States of the Union are being harmonised with a view to the introduction of a single currency. It was the subject of one of the two Intergovernmental Conferences held in December 1990. The Treaty provides that EMU is to be achieved in three stages:

— first stage (1 July 1990 to 31 December 1993): free movement of capital between Member States, closer coordination of economic policies and closer cooperation between central banks;
— second stage (1 January 1994 to 31 December 1998): convergence of the economic and monetary policies of the Member States (to ensure stability of prices and sound public finances);
— third stage (from 1 January 1999): establishment of a European Central Bank, fixing of exchange rates and introduction of a single currency.

Eleven Member States are participating in the third stage of EMU that began on 1 January 1999. Four Member States have not adopted the single currency, either because they decided not to — under the protocols annexed to the EC Treaty granting them the option (United Kingdom and Denmark) — or because they failed to meet the convergence criteria laid down by the Treaty of Maastricht (Greece and Sweden).

Economic and social cohesion

The origins of economic and social cohesion go back to the Treaty of Rome where a reference is made in the preamble to reducing disparities in development between the regions. However, it was not until the 1970s that Community action was taken to coordinate the national instruments and provide additional financial resources. Subsequently these measures proved inadequate given the situation in the Community where the establishment of the internal market, contrary to forecasts, had failed to even out the differences between regions.

With the adoption of the Single European Act in 1986, economic and social cohesion proper was made an objective, as well as the single market. In the preparation of economic and monetary union, this provided a legal basis from 1988 onwards for Community action to become the central pillar of a comprehensive development policy.

The Maastricht Treaty finally incorporated the policy into the Treaty establishing the European Community (Articles 130a to 130e, now renumbered 158 to 162). It is an expression of solidarity between the Member States and regions of the European Union. This means balanced and sustainable development, reducing structural disparities between regions and countries and promoting equal opportunities for all individuals. In practical terms it is achieved by means of a variety of financing operations, principally through the Structural Funds.

Every three years the European Commission must present a report on progress made in achieving economic and social cohesion and on how the various means provided for in the Treaty have contributed to it.

The future of economic and social cohesion was one of the major issues discussed in the Commission's Agenda 2000 communication (presented on 15 July 1997), largely because of the financial implications. It has been the Community's second largest budget item from 1994 to 1999 (around 35 % of the budget). Its importance was confirmed in the financial perspective 2000–06.

With enlargement looking set to bring in countries with national incomes well below the Community average, the Community structural policy was reformed in 1999 in order to improve its effectiveness and its budgetary allocation has been increased from EUR 208 billion to EUR 213 billion for 2000–06.

Economic and Social Committee

The Economic and Social Committee consists of 222 members falling into three categories: employers, workers and representatives of particular types of activity (such as farmers, craftsmen, the professions, consumer representatives, scientists and teachers, cooperatives, families, environmental movements). Members are appointed for four years by unanimous Council decision. The Committee is consulted before a great many acts are adopted, and it may also issue opinions on its own initiative.

Following the entry into force of the Treaty of Amsterdam, the Committee has to be consulted on an even wider range of issues (the new employment policy, social affairs, public health) and may also be consulted by the European Parliament.

Economic policy

National economic policies are identified in the Treaty as a matter of common concern requiring a degree of coordination within the Council to help attain the Community's objectives.

In practical terms, the Council, acting by a qualified majority on a recommendation from the Commission, formulates draft guidelines which are sent to the European Council. In the light of that body's conclusions, the Council, again by qualified majority, adopts a recommendation setting out the broad guidelines of the economic policies of the Member States and the Community and informs the European Parliament (Article 99(2) of the EC Treaty).

However, the economic policy provisions of Articles 98 to 104 (former Articles 102a to 104c) also allow for several other procedures depending on the matter in hand:

— the cooperation procedure for questions relating to multilateral surveillance (Art. 99(5)), the application of the prohibition of privileged access (Art. 102(2)), the application of the prohibition of the assumption of commitments and the granting of overdraft facilities (Art. 103(2));
— simple consultation with a qualified majority in the Council in the case of provisions on the application of the protocol on the excessive deficit procedure (Art. 104(14), third subparagraph);
— unanimity in the Council without consultation, for measures appropriate to the economic situation (100(1));
— qualified majority in the Council, Commission report, opinion of the Monetary Committee, Commission opinion and recommendation (taking into account the observations of the Member State concerned), to decide whether an excessive deficit exists (Art. 104(6));
— two thirds of the votes in the Council (excluding those of the Member State concerned) on a recommendation from the Commission for the excessive deficit procedure (Art. 104(13));
— unanimity in the Council (except in the case of natural disasters) on a proposal from the Commission in the case of Community financial assistance to a Member State in severe economic difficulties (100(2)); Parliament must be informed.

The institutional provisions (Articles 112–115) and transitional provisions (Articles 116–124) of Title VII of the EC Treaty (economic and monetary policy — former Title VI) have their own special decision-making procedures, separate from those listed here.

Education, vocational training and youth

European Community action in the fields of education and training dates back to 1976. However, it was the Maastricht Treaty which provided a legal basis in Articles 149 and 150 (formerly Articles 126 and 127) of the Treaty establishing the European Community. These provisions, which were not substantially changed by the Treaty of Amsterdam, lay down that measures relating to education and vocational training are to be adopted under the co-decision procedure following consultation of the Economic and Social Committee and the Committee of the Regions.

Since 1995 there have been three main education and vocational training programmes.

— Socrates encourages student mobility, and to that end, cooperation between universities (Erasmus programme), schools (Comenius programme) and in language learning (Lingua programme). Socrates also encourages the development of networks with a view to the recognition of qualifications, the provision of information in the field of education (Eurydice) and the exchange of experience between decision-makers in the field of education (Arion);
— Leonardo da Vinci promotes access to vocational training by improving national vocational training systems and encouraging innovation and life-long learning;
— Youth for Europe III facilitates the mobility of less privileged young people outside education structures in order to give them access to local projects which complement their training as citizens.

Finally, a European voluntary service programme was set up in 1997 to enable young Europeans to participate in projects of varying lengths run by associations or local authorities in Europe or developing countries. However, it does not replace Member States' national services.

With regard to trans-European cooperation, since 1990 the Tempus programme has been encouraging exchanges in the field of higher education between the European Union and the countries of central and eastern Europe, the former Soviet republics and Mongolia. It is financed by Union programmes, namely Phare and Tacis, which promote the economic and social restructuring of those countries.

Besides action taken by the Community itself, the Commission has created two structures to support Union activities in the field of vocational training:

— the European Centre for the Development of Vocational Training (Cedefop): set up in 1975 and based in Thessaloniki, it develops academic and technical activities in support of the development of vocational training in Europe;
— the European Training Foundation: set up in 1995 and based in Turin, it supports and coordinates the reform of vocational training systems as part of Phare, Tacis and MEDA.

Without impinging on the powers of the Member States in the field of education, the Union aims to give everyone the possibility of training or further education throughout their life. Helping the active population to adapt continuously to technological change is one of the main tools in the fight against unemployment and in building a genuine Europe of knowledge.

Employment

Employment is one of the key concerns of the Member States, for unemployment is running at a high level (currently around 11 % in the Union). Following on from the Commission's 1993 White Paper on growth, competitiveness and employment, the Essen European Council (9 and 10 December 1994) identified five priority areas for action to promote employment:

— improving employment opportunities by promoting investment in vocational training;
— increasing the employment-intensiveness of growth;
— reducing non-wage labour costs;
— increasing the effectiveness of labour-market policies;
— improving help for groups which are particularly hard hit by unemployment.

The Council and the Commission presented a joint report on the action taken on these five priorities at the Dublin European Council (13 and 14 December 1996).

Similarly the Confidence Pact for Employment presented by the Commission President in June 1996 seeks to mobilise all the actors concerned in a genuine strategy for employment, to make employment a matter of common interest at European level and incorporate the fight against unemployment in a medium and long-term vision of society.

With the entry into force of the Treaty of Amsterdam, employment is now enshrined as one of the European Community's objectives. The Community has been assigned the new responsibility of working towards a coordinated strategy for employment together with the Member States. To this end, a new title on employment (Title VIII) has been written into the EC Treaty, under which:

— employment to be taken into consideration in other Community policies;
— coordination mechanisms to be established at Community level (adoption by the Council of guidelines for employment and surveillance of their implementation in the Member States, creation of an advisory committee on employment);
— the possibility for the Council, acting by a qualified majority, to adopt incentive measures, including pilot projects (in addition to the Structural Funds).

An extraordinary summit on employment was held on 21 November 1997, focusing on employability, entrepreneurship, adaptability and equal opportunities. The Member States then decided to bring forward to 1998 the application of the provisions on coordinating their employment policies.

Employment Committee

Set up by the Treaty of Amsterdam, the advisory Employment Committee has replaced the Employment and Labour Market Committee set up in 1996 (Article 130 of the EC Treaty).

Made up of two representatives of each Member State and two representatives of the Commission, the Committee's task is to assist the Council with its responsibilities in these fields. It monitors Member States' employment and labour market policies, promotes their coordination and delivers opinions. In performing its remit it consults the social partners (management and labour).

Enlargement

Enlargement or widening is the term used to refer to the four successive waves of new members joining the Community. Nine countries have so far joined the six founder members — Belgium, France, Germany, Italy, Luxembourg and the Netherlands — at the following times:

— 1973: Denmark, Ireland and the United Kingdom;
— 1981: Greece;
— 1986: Portugal and Spain;
— 1995: Austria, Finland and Sweden.

With the growing number of applicants for membership, the concept of enlargement has taken on a very special significance. There is a widespread conviction that the system established by the Treaty of Rome cannot function effectively in a Union of 25 to 30 members without a reform of the institutions and certain Union policies. Since then, debate has centred on the terms 'enlargement' and 'deepening'. Some believe that there can be no question of increasing the number of members without a complete overhaul of the institutions and of the way the European Union operates. Others maintain that enlargement is the priority (the thought in the back of their minds often being that it will water down the Union's political aspirations).

Under the Treaty of Amsterdam, a protocol on the institutions was annexed to the EU Treaty, requiring a new intergovernmental conference to be convened at least one year before the membership of the Union exceeds 20. Its task will be to settle the institutional problems relating to enlargement, in particular the weighting of votes and the composition of the Commission. It has been argued that the extension of qualified majority voting is an indispensable condition for the smooth functioning of the institutions in an enlarged Europe (see the joint declaration by Belgium, France and Italy attached to the Final Act of the Intergovernmental Conference).

On 15 July 1997 the Commission adopted Agenda 2000, a document which is closely bound up with enlargement and deals with all the issues facing the European Union at the beginning of the 21st century.

Environment

The aim of Community environment policy is to preserve, protect and improve the quality of the environment and to protect people's health. It also sets great store by the prudent and rational use of natural resources. Lastly, it seeks to promote measures at international level to deal with regional or worldwide environmental problems (Article 174, formerly Article 130r).

Policy formulation is subject to different decision-making procedures depending on the area concerned. So to attain the objectives listed in Article 174, the Council:

— acts under the cooperation procedure, after consulting the Economic and Social Committee, for decisions on the measures to be taken and on the implementation of programmes;
— acts unanimously, after consulting the European Parliament and the Economic and Social Committee, where fiscal provisions and provisions relating to town and country planning or land use (with the exception of waste management and general measures) are involved or where a Member State's choice in the matter of energy is significantly affected (Article 175(2), formerly Article 130s(2)) (under this procedure the Council may also define matters referred to in Article 175(2), on which decisions are taken by a qualified majority);
— acts under the co-decision procedure, after consulting the Economic and Social Committee, for the adoption of general action programmes setting out the priority objectives to be attained.

The Treaty of Amsterdam has enshrined the concept of 'sustainable development' as one of the European Union's objectives, while environmental protection requirements have been given greater weight in other Community policies, especially in the context of the single market.

The provisions allowing a Member State to apply stricter rules than the harmonised rules have been clarified and doing so has been made easier. Under certain narrowly defined conditions, a Member State may now adopt new measures in response to a specific environmental problem.

The Commission monitors these stricter measures to ensure that they do not constitute an obstacle to the functioning of the single market. The Commission itself has undertaken to prepare environmental impact assessments when making proposals that may have significant environmental implications.

Lastly, decision-making has been simplified, with the co-decision procedure replacing the cooperation procedure that was previously required in certain cases.

Equal opportunities

Two key elements of the general principle of equal opportunities are the ban on discrimination on grounds of nationality (Article 12 of the EC Treaty, formerly Article 6) and equal pay for men and women (Article 141 of the EC Treaty, formerly Article 119). It is intended to apply to all fields, particularly economic, social, cultural and family life.

The Treaty of Amsterdam added a new Article 13 to the Treaty, reinforcing the principle of non-discrimination, which is closely linked to equal opportunities. Under this new Article, the Council has the power to take appropriate action to combat discrimination based on sex, racial or ethnic origin, religion or belief, disability, age or sexual orientation.

Equal treatment for men and women

As early as 1957, Article 141 (former Article 119) of the EC Treaty laid down the principle that men and women should receive equal pay for equal work. Since 1975 a series of directives have broadened the principle to cover access to employment, training and career progression and working conditions, the aim being to eliminate all forms of discrimination at work. Equal treatment was later extended to social security, statutory schemes and occupational schemes. In the 1980s recognition of this principle led to the promotion of equal opportunities via multiannual programmes.

The Treaty of Amsterdam seeks to supplement Article 141 (which is rather limited in scope, covering only equal pay) by including the promotion of equality between men and women as one of the tasks of the Community set out in Article 2 of the EC Treaty.

Eurocorps

Eurocorps was set up at the 59th Franco-German summit, which took place in La Rochelle on 21 and 22 May 1992. Three other countries have since joined it: Belgium on 25 June 1993, Spain on 10 December 1993 and Luxembourg on 7 May 1996. It comprises 50 000 men and has been operational since 30 November 1995, following the Pegasus-95 exercise.

Eurocorps forms part of the Forces answerable to Western European Union (FAWEU). It can operate as such within WEU (Article V) or NATO (Article 5) and can be mobilised for humanitarian missions, missions to evacuate Member State nationals and peace-restoring or peacekeeping operations, under the aegis of the United Nations or the OSCE. The commitment of Eurocorps under the political control of WEU was the subject of an agreement signed on 24 September 1993 and commitment under NATO authority was codified by the agreement of 21 January 1993.

Eurofor/Euromarfor

The Lisbon Declaration of the Western European Union on 15 May 1995 ratified the decision by Spain, France and Italy to set up land and sea forces (Eurofor and Euromarfor). These will form part of the forces answerable to WEU (FAWEU) and should strengthen Europe's own capacity for operations under the Petersberg Declaration. Portugal has agreed to participate in the two forces when they are being used within the WEU context, without prejudice to the Member States' collective defence position (Article V, WEU, and Article 5, NATO).

Europe agreement

A Europe agreement is a specific type of association agreement concluded between the European Union and certain central and eastern European States. Its aim is to prepare the associated State for accession to the European Union, and is based on respect of human rights, democracy, the rule of law and the market economy. To date, Europe agreements have been concluded with 10 countries: Bulgaria, the Czech Republic, Estonia, Hungary, Latvia, Lithuania, Poland, Romania, Slovakia and Slovenia (the Slovene agreement was signed on 10 June 1996 but has not yet come into force).

A Europe agreement is concluded for an indefinite period and is made up of a number of elements:

— a political aspect, providing for bilateral and multilateral consultations on any questions of common interest;
— a trade aspect, in order to set up a free trade area;
— economic, cultural and financial cooperation;
— alignment of legislation, particularly on intellectual property and competition rules.

As regards the institutional arrangements, the general management of a Europe agreement is the responsibility of an Association Council, made up of representatives of the Council and the Commission on the one hand and representatives of the associated State's government on the other. An Association Committee, made up of members of the Association Council, follows up the work and prepares the discussions of the Association Council. Finally, a Parliamentary Association Committee, made up of Members of the European Parliament and of the national parliament of the Associated State, may make recommendations to the Association Council.

Europe 'à la carte'

This refers to the idea of a non-uniform method of integration which allows Member States to select policies as if from a menu and involve themselves fully in those policies; there would still be a minimum number of common objectives.

European Central Bank (ECB)

The European Central Bank was inaugurated on 30 June 1998. On 1 January 1999 it took over responsibility for implementing European monetary policy as defined by the European System of Central Banks (ESCB). As to the practicalities, the ECB's decision-making bodies (the Governing Council and the Executive Board) run the European System of Central Banks, whose tasks are to manage the money in circulation, conduct foreign-exchange operations, hold and manage the Member States' official foreign reserves, and promote the smooth operation of payment systems. The ECB took over from its precursor, the European Monetary Institute (EMI).

European Commission

The European Commission is a body with powers of initiative, implementation, management and control. It is the guardian of the treaties and the embodiment of the interests of the Community. It is composed of 20 independent members (two each from France, Germany, Italy, Spain and the United Kingdom and one each from all the other countries). It is appointed for a five-year term, by agreement among the Member States, and is subject to a vote of appointment by the European Parliament, to which it is answerable, before it can be sworn in. The Commissioners are assisted by an administration made up of directorates-general and specialised departments whose staff are divided mainly between Brussels and Luxembourg.

In adopting the Treaty of Amsterdam, the Intergovernmental Conference took note of the Commission's intention to prepare a reorganisation of tasks among the Commissioners before the next Commission takes up office in 2000 and at the same time to embark on a corresponding reorganisation of its departments.

The European Commission tackled the question of reforming its internal procedures in Agenda 2000, a document it adopted on 15 July 1997, which refers to the far-reaching programme of reforms already under way at the Commission under the SEM 2000 (Sound and Efficient Management) and MAP 2000 (Modernisation of Administration and Personnel Policy) initiatives and stresses the need for the Commission to regroup and redefine its tasks, taking into account the needs of the 21st century.

European Conference

The European Conference was set up to provide a framework for the enlargement process over the next few years, bringing together the Member States of the European Union with the European countries that are hoping to join. It is a multilateral forum for political consultation on questions of general interest, particularly:

— the common foreign and security policy;
— justice and home affairs;
— economic affairs and regional cooperation.

It was launched by the Luxembourg European Council in December 1997, taking up a French initiative presented in October 1997. It meets once a year at the level of Heads of State or Government and the President of the Commission, and once a year at foreign minister level. It is chaired by the country which holds the presidency of the Council of the European Union.

The European Conference met for the first time in London on 12 March 1998 and decided to set up a joint group of experts charged with reporting on the growing problems that organised crime poses for European societies, particularly in eastern Europe. The first meeting at ministerial level was held on 6 October 1998 in Luxembourg.

European Convention on Human Rights (ECHR)

A European Convention on Human Rights signed in Rome under the aegis of the Council of Europe on 4 November 1950 established an unprecedented system of international protection for human rights, offering individuals the possibility of applying to the courts for the enforcement of their rights. The convention, which has been ratified by all the Member States of the Union, established a number of supervisory bodies based in Strasbourg. These were:

— a Commission responsible for advance examination of applications from States or from individuals;
— a European Court of Human Rights, to which cases were referred by the Commission or by a Member State following a report by the Commission (in the case of a judicial settlement);
— a Committee of Ministers of the Council of Europe which acted as the guardian of the ECHR and to which reference was made, where a case was not brought before the Court, to secure political settlement of a dispute.

The growing number of cases made it necessary to reform the supervisory arrangements established by the convention (addition of Protocol No 11). The supervisory bodies were thus replaced on 1 November 1998, by a single European Court of Human Rights. The simplified structure shortened the length of procedures and enhanced the judicial character of the system.

The idea of the European Union acceding to the ECHR has often been raised. However, in an opinion given on 28 March 1996, the European Court of Justice stated that the European Communities could not accede to the convention because the EC Treaty does not provide any powers to lay down rules or to conclude international agreements in the matter of human rights. Thus, for the moment, accession depends on the Treaty being amended.

The Treaty of Amsterdam nevertheless calls for respect for the fundamental rights guaranteed by the convention, while formalising the judgments of the Court of Justice on the matter. With regard to relations between the two Courts, the practice developed by the Court of Justice of incorporating the principles of the convention into Union law has made it possible to maintain coherence in their work and their independence.

European Council

The European Council is the term used to describe the regular meetings of the Heads of State or Government of the European Union Member States. It was set up by the communiqué issued at the close of the December 1974 Paris summit and first met in 1975 (in Dublin, on 10 and 11 March). Before that time, from 1961 to 1974, the practice had been to hold European summit conferences. Its existence was given legal recognition by the Single European Act, while official status was conferred on it by the Treaty on European Union. It meets at least twice a year and the President of the European Commission attends as a full member. Its objectives are to give the European Union the impetus it needs in order to develop further and to define general policy guidelines.

European Parliament

The European Parliament is the assembly of the representatives of the 370 million Union citizens. Since 1979 they have been elected by direct universal suffrage and today total 626 distributed between Member States by reference to their population. Parliament's main functions are as follows:

— it considers the Commission's proposals and is associated with the Council in the legislative process by means of various procedures (co-decision, cooperation, etc.);
— it has the power of control over the Union's activities through its confirmation of the appointment of the Commission (and the right to censure it) and through the written and oral questions it can put to the Commission and the Council;
— it shares budgetary powers with the Council in voting on the annual budget and overseeing its implementation.

It also appoints an Ombudsman empowered to receive complaints from Union citizens concerning maladministration in the activities of the Community institutions or bodies. Finally, it can set up temporary committees of inquiry, whose powers are not confined to examining the actions of the Community institutions but may also relate to actions by Member States in implementing Community policies.

The Treaty of Amsterdam has simplified the various legislative procedures by virtually doing away with the cooperation procedure (it still applies in a few cases coming under the Title on economic and monetary union) and considerably extending the co-decision procedure.

Europol (European Police Office)

The idea of a European Police Office was first raised at the Luxembourg European Council on 28 and 29 June 1991. The plan then was to set up a new body which would provide a structure for developing police cooperation between Member States in preventing and combating serious forms of international organised crime, including terrorism and drug trafficking. The convention establishing Europol was signed in July 1995 and entered into force on 1 October 1998.

In order to lose no time in giving practical shape to the police cooperation defined in Title VI of the Treaty on European Union, a temporary Europol Drugs Unit was set up in 1995. The prime objective of this Unit was to combat drug trafficking and associated money laundering. Its terms of reference were subsequently extended to cover measures to combat trafficking in radioactive and nuclear substances, clandestine immigration networks, vehicle trafficking and money laundering associated with these criminal activities; the fight against trade in human beings was also added later. The European Police Office, which took over the activities of the Europol Drugs Unit, became operational on 1 July 1999.

Europol, which has its headquarters in The Hague, works in the same fields and, since 1 January 1999, also has powers to combat terrorism and money counterfeiting.

The Treaty of Amsterdam confers a number of different tasks on Europol: coordinating and implementing specific investigations conducted by the Member States' authorities, developing specialised expertise in order to help Member States in their investigations into organised crime, and establishing contacts with prosecutors and investigators who specialise in the fight against organised crime.

European political cooperation (EPC)

European political cooperation (EPC) was introduced informally in 1970 (in response to the Davignon report) and formalised by the Single European Act with effect from 1987. The object is consultations between the Member States in foreign policy matters. The Member States have regard for the views of the European Parliament and wherever possible take common positions in international organisations. EPC was superseded by the common foreign and security policy.

European security and defence identity

The idea of developing a European defence identity has been prompted by two considerations.

— For some years now Europe has been faced with the emergence of several hotbeds of instability in the eastern half of the continent, such as Bosnia-Herzegovina and Kosovo.
— The relative decline in the United States' defence commitment has left a void which Europe has not succeeded in filling. The last few years have consequently served to emphasise the limitations of an alliance (NATO) which defines itself primarily in relation to an external threat. At the same time there is a growing realisation of the need for a political entity motivated by an awareness of shared interests to face up to the new security challenges in Europe.

Against this background, the NATO Council held in Brussels in January 1994 recognised the importance of defining a specifically European identity in relation to security and defence. The first steps towards this were taken at the NATO Council held in Berlin on 3 June 1996 with the development of the concept of Combined Joint Task Forces (CJTF), to which the Ministers of the Alliance subscribed at the January 1994 summit as a means of using NATO's military capacity in operations led by the WEU under its political control and strategic management. Europe will also have elements within NATO's military structure carrying out command functions and wearing two hats: NATO's and Europe's. European command dispositions of this kind should be identifiable and sufficiently well structured to ensure that a militarily coherent and effective operational force can be put together at speed.

External responsibilities of the European Community

The European Community's external responsibilities are defined in accordance with whether they are conferred on the Community or on the Member States. They are described as 'exclusive' where they are exercised entirely by the Community (e.g. the common agricultural policy) and 'mixed' where they are shared with the Member States (e.g. the transport policy).

The distinction has been defined in Court of Justice case law and is based on the principle of implicit responsibility, whereby external responsibility derives from the existence of internal responsibility. The

Treaty confers explicit responsibility in only two cases: commercial policy (Article 133, formerly Article 113) and association agreements (Article 310, formerly Article 238).

It should be pointed out that the common foreign and security policy comes under the heading of the EU's external relations, which are governed by intergovernmental procedures (second pillar), rather than under the external responsibilities of the European Community.

The growth in the Community's activities (e.g. the completion of the single market), developments in world trade and the less clear-cut case law have made the exercise of external powers more problematic, while at the same time entailing a far-reaching duty to cooperate and coordinate in the name of a united front in international representation.

To enable the Community to adapt to the radical changes in the structures of the world economy and reflect the wide responsibilities given to the World Trade Organisation, the Treaty of Amsterdam has amended Article 133 of the EC Treaty to allow the Council, acting unanimously, to broaden the scope of the common commercial policy to cover international negotiations and agreements on services and intellectual property.

F

Fight against drugs

The fight against drugs involves a wide range of activities, chief among them the fight against addiction and illicit trafficking. The European Union can rely on various specific legal bases for action.

Preventing drug addiction comes under Article 152 of the EC Treaty (public health — former Article 129). Measures taken by the Community on this basis include an action programme for 1996–2000.

Responsibility for combating illicit drug trafficking rests with the Europol Drugs Unit, which has set up an intelligence unit to improve police and customs cooperation between the Member States. On 1 October 1998 the unit became part of the European Police Office.

The Treaty of Amsterdam clearly identifies the fight against illicit drug trafficking as one of the objectives of the new Title VI of the EU Treaty (police and judicial cooperation in criminal matters). On the basis of Article 29 (former Article K.1) of the Treaty on European Union, the Commission adopted a Union action plan against drugs (2000–04). This plan makes the fight against drugs one of the Union's internal and external priorities. In order to equip the EU with the necessary tools, it recommends exchanging reliable data and stepping up international cooperation.

Fight against fraud

The fight against fraud and corruption rests on two separate legal bases, both of which were amended by the Treaty of Amsterdam:

— Article 29 of the EU Treaty calls for 'closer cooperation between police forces, customs authorities and other competent authorities in the Member States, both directly and through Europol' in this area;
— Article 280 of the EC Treaty concerns activities affecting the Community's financial interests. Here, the Council and the European Parliament have the power to adopt measures under the co-decision procedure after consulting the Court of Auditors.

A convention on the protection of the Community's financial interests was signed on 26 July 1995 as a third-pillar instrument. Its principal aim is that there should be provision in the criminal law of all Member States for an offence of fraud against the Community's financial interests. Since 1988, this type of fraud was tackled by the European Commission's fraud prevention task force (UCLAF) which was replaced by the European Anti-fraud Office (OLAF) on 1 June 1999.

Fight against international organised crime and money-laundering

The Europol Drugs Unit has been made responsible for fighting these two scourges; it exchanges information between Member States to improve police and judicial cooperation. On 1 October 1998, the new European Police Office (Europol) took over the responsibilities of the Drugs Unit, a temporary structure put in place in 1994 pending the entry into force of the Europol Convention.

The fight against international crime is one of the fields included in the new Title VI of the EU Treaty. This explicit reference enables the Member States to go beyond the mere exchange of information, as they now have a clear legal basis for embarking on a genuine policy to combat international crime, using the instruments available under the new Article 34 (common positions, decisions, framework decisions and conventions).

During the Amsterdam European Council in June 1997, the political will of the Member States in the fight against organised crime was translated into action by the adoption of an action programme setting the European Union's priorities. In addition, a pre-accession pact on organised crime was signed on 28 May 1998 with the applicant countries.

Fight against racism and xenophobia

Before the entry into force of the Amsterdam Treaty, various measures against racism and xenophobia had been taken within the framework of social policy. For instance, a Council resolution declared 1997 the European Year against Racism, but it was left to the Member States to take practical action.

On 25 March 1998, after Parliament had passed several resolutions on the subject, the Commission presented an action plan against racism to consolidate what had been achieved during 1997 and to prepare the ground for the entry into force of the Treaty of Amsterdam. One of the aims is to incorporate the fight against racism into Community policies and programmes.

The Amsterdam Treaty, in the shape of Article 29 (former Article K.1) of the Treaty on European Union, provides a specific legal basis for preventing and combating racism and xenophobia. It opens up the possibility of a genuine Union policy in this matter.

A European Monitoring Centre for Racism and Xenophobia was set up in Vienna in June 1997 for the purpose of exchanging information and experience in this area. On 21 December 1998 an agreement was concluded between the Centre and the Council of Europe in order to step up cooperation between the Centre and the Council of Europe Committee on racism and intolerance.

Fight against terrorism

The Treaty of Amsterdam has inserted a specific reference to the fight against terrorism into Article 29 of the EU Treaty (former Article K.1), thereby allowing the Member States to adopt common positions, decisions, framework decisions and conventions in order to establish closer coordination in this field.

It also assigned the task of coordinating the fight against terrorism to the European Police Office (Europol). With the Europol Convention having come into force on 1 October 1998, police cooperation on terrorism under the auspices of Europol began on 1 January 1999.

Financial perspective 2000–06

The financial perspective forms the framework for Community expenditure over a period of several years. It is the product of an interinstitutional agreement between the European Parliament, the Council and the Commission and indicates the maximum volume and the composition of the foreseeable Community expenditure. It is adjusted annually by the Commission to take account of prices and the development of Community GNP. However, it should be noted that the financial perspective is not a multi-annual budget, since the annual budgetary procedure remains essential to determine the actual amount of expenditure and the breakdown between the different budget headings.

To date, three interinstitutional agreements of this type have been concluded, the first in 1988, the second in 1992 and the third in 1999:

— the 1988–92 financial perspective (Delors I package);
— the 1993–99 financial perspective (Delors II package);
— the 2000–06 financial perspective.

The financial perspective 2000–06 is part of the new Interinstitutional Agreement which is the cornerstone of the Agenda 2000 financial package. This Agreement, which received political endorsement at the Berlin Summit in March 1999, should enable the Union to take in new members and at the same time strengthen its policies while keeping to a rigorous financial framework.

The financial perspective establishes the reference framework for a period of seven years (2000–06). Although it cannot incorporate expenditure linked to new accessions before they take effect, it does, nonetheless, have three features that are interesting in terms of enlargement.

— Agricultural funding is extended to encompass a new rural development policy, veterinary measures, a pre-accession agricultural instrument, and a margin left available for enlargement.
— The allocation for the Structural Funds destined for the 15 Member States will be gradually reduced from 2002 onwards by concentrating the priorities on a more limited number of regions. Structural operations also comprise a new pre-accession instrument.
— The amount allocated for external action is increased by 2 % per year so as to cover the increase in pre-accession aid under the Phare programme. In addition, the allocations provided for pre-accession aid (Phare, ISPA and Sapard) will remain unchanged irrespective of the number of applicant countries which will become members of the European Union during the period 2000–06. Resources can thus be concentrated on the countries in greatest need.

Lastly, budgetary discipline will make it possible to maintain the current ceiling on expenditure, 1.27 % of the Community's GNP, until 2006.

Free movement of persons (visas, asylum, immigration and other policies)

The Treaty of Amsterdam has written a new Title IV into the EC Treaty. It covers the following fields:

— free movement of persons;
— controls on external borders;
— asylum, immigration and safeguarding of the rights of third-country nationals;
— judicial cooperation in civil matters.

These fields used to come under Title VI of the EU Treaty (Justice and home affairs). But now the Treaty of Amsterdam has 'communitised' them, in other words brought them under the legal framework of the first pillar, and they will gradually be incorporated over a period of five years following its entry into force.

After this transition period, the Council will no longer act alone in these fields but will take decisions on a proposal from the Commission, the eventual aim being to apply the co-decision procedure and qualified majority voting. Moreover, the Court of Justice now has jurisdiction in the fields covered by the new Title IV.

The United Kingdom and Ireland have opted out of measures taken under Title IV. Denmark will participate only in measures relating to visas.

G

General-interest services

General-interest services are services considered to be in the general interest by the public authorities and accordingly subjected to specific public-service obligations. They include non-market services (e.g. compulsory education, social protection), obligations of the State (e.g. security and justice) and services of general economic interest (e.g. energy and communications). Article 86 of the Treaty (former Article 90) does not apply to the first two categories (non-market services and State obligations).

Globalisation of the economy

The phenomenon of economic globalisation was identified by the Turin European Council as one of the major challenges facing the European Union at the end of the 20th century. The term refers to a process of growing economic integration worldwide, and the main driving forces behind it are:

— the liberalisation of international trade and capital movements;
— accelerating technological progress and the advent of the information society;
— deregulation.

These three factors accentuate each other: technological progress stimulates international trade and worldwide patterns of trade allow for more effective dissemination of technological progress. At the same time, deregulation stimulates the development of new forms of technology and contributes to removing barriers to trade. Some observers, however, blame technological progress for enabling businesses and individuals to find a way round national regulations more easily.

Green Paper

Commission Green Papers are documents intended to stimulate debate and launch a process of consultation at European level on a particular topic (such as social policy, the single currency, telecommunications). These consultations may then lead to the publication of a White Paper, translating the conclusions of the debate into practical proposals for Community action.

H

Hard core

This refers to a small group of countries able and willing to enter into closer cooperation with one another. This concept has to be seen in the wider context of flexibility, which should see differentiated integration enshrined in the institutional framework of the Union to prevent hard cores from forming outside this framework (as was the case with the Schengen area).

Hierarchy of Community acts (hierarchy of norms)

A declaration annexed to the Treaty on European Union states that, 'it might be possible to review the classification of Community acts with a view to establishing an appropriate hierarchy between the different categories of act.'

The main purpose of such a hierarchy would be to enable the lawmaking authority to concentrate on political aspects of particular issues rather than on questions of detail. It would dictate the shape of the Community decision-making process by ensuring that instruments of constitutional status were subject to tougher procedures (such as adoption by unanimous vote or by augmented qualified majority, and assent) than legislative instruments, which are themselves subject to tougher procedures (for example, the co-decision procedure) than implementing instruments (for instance, the institutionalised delegation of powers to the Commission).

The subject was addressed in 1990 in the early discussions on the possibility of inserting the co-decision procedure into the Treaty. The underlying idea was to avoid an over-rigorous procedure being applied to certain acts of secondary importance and thereby prevent the legislative machinery becoming congested. In 1991, during the negotiations on the Treaty of Maastricht, the Commission proposed introducing a hierarchy of acts and a new system for classifying Communities instruments (treaties, laws, secondary or implementing acts), but failed to overcome the different national legal traditions. The issue was not raised in the negotiations at the 1996–97 Intergovernmental Conference.

High Representative for the CFSP

Following the debate on whether to appoint a 'Mr/Ms CFSP', a new position of High Representative for the common foreign and security policy has now been created by the Treaty of Amsterdam. The new position is held by the Secretary-General of the Council, whose task is to assist the Presidency of the Union in matters relating to the common foreign and security policy.

The High Representative also helps in formulating, preparing and implementing policy decisions by the Council. He or she may conduct political dialogue with third parties, on the Council's behalf and at the request of the Presidency.

Responsibility for running the Council's General Secretariat now rests with the Deputy Secretary-General.

Human rights

The case law of the Court of Justice of the European Communities recognises the principles laid down in the Council of Europe's Convention on Human Rights. This respect for human rights was confirmed by the Member States in the preamble to the 1986 Single Act and later incorporated into Article 6 (former Article F) of the EU Treaty, which is based on the above convention and the shared constitutional traditions of the Member States.

The guarantee of respect for fundamental rights has been further strengthened by the Treaty of Amsterdam, which has extended the jurisdiction of the Court of Justice to cover respect for the rights deriving from Article 6 with regard to action by the Union institutions. At the same time, a new suspension clause lays down what action is to be taken in cases where a Member State breaches the principles on which the Union is founded.

Incorporation of the Community *acquis*

The Essen European Council (December 1994) called on the Commission to present a White Paper on the preparation of the associated countries of central and eastern Europe for integration into the Union's internal market, which it did at the Cannes European Council in June 1995. The White Paper contains an indicative programme for the alignment of the central and eastern European countries' legislation with that of the internal market. It provides that these countries will establish priorities in order to incorporate the Community rules and that they will be helped in this work by a technical assistance office (TAIEX), particularly in order to obtain information on Community legislation.

The incorporation and implementation of all Community legislation are the main challenges which the applicant countries face. They require the administrations and the legal systems to be strengthened, and the infrastructure of the applicant countries to be drastically adapted to conform to Community standards, particularly on environmental questions, and to develop genuine transport, energy and telecommunications networks. To facilitate these considerable adjustments, pre-accession aid is provided to the applicant countries.

The accession negotiations for the 11 applicant countries designated by the Luxembourg European Council (December 1997) began on 30 March 1998 following the European Conference. The first step is to evaluate each applicant country's legislation for compatibility with the Community rules (screening process). This evaluation will then constitute the basis for the second stage, bilateral negotiations between the Union and each applicant. It will be possible for the applicants to ask for transition periods between their accession and the time when they are capable of fully implementing Community legislation. However, any such transition periods must be as short as possible and confined to specific sectors.

Incorporation of the Social Policy Agreement (abolition of the Social Policy Protocol)

The Treaty of Amsterdam has done away with the Social Policy Protocol, the mechanism by which the United Kingdom allowed the other Member States to advance on the social policy front without taking part itself. Following the statement by the new British Government that it intended to join forces with the other Member States on social policy, it was decided to incorporate the Social Policy Agreement into the EC Treaty.

The United Kingdom has two years to implement the directives adopted by the other 14 Member States under the Social Policy Agreement. In actual practice, the British opt-out from social policy was lifted in 1997, well before the entry into force of the Treaty of Amsterdam and the formal abolition of the Social Policy Protocol.

Industry

Industry has been the subject of a specific article in the EC Treaty since 1993, when the EU Treaty came into force. Article 157 (former Article 130) requires the Community and the Member States to secure the conditions necessary for the competitiveness of Community industry.

Specific measures may be taken by the Community, but only on condition that they do not entail any distortion of competition. The Community is also required to contribute towards achieving the objectives of Article 157 through the policies and activities it pursues under other provisions of the Treaty.

In terms of decision-making, the Council acts unanimously on a Commission proposal, after consulting the European Parliament and the Economic and Social Committee.

In March 1995, the Commission presented an action programme with four priority areas intended to promote industrial competitiveness:

— strengthening the internal market;
— taking industrial needs into account in research policy;
— development of the information society;
— promotion of industrial cooperation.

Institutional balance and democratic legitimacy

The Community's institutional balance has for a long time been State-based, with the Member States acting as virtually the sole driving force behind European integration. As this process of construction has developed, the question of legitimacy has become more and more acute. Thus the Treaty of Maastricht sparked off the incorporation of the principle of democratic legitimacy into the heart of the institutional system by giving the European Parliament greater powers over the appointment and supervision of the Commission.

Despite the steps forward taken by the Treaty on European Union, there is still an imbalance between the Council's legislative powers and those of Parliament. The process of ratifying the Treaty in the Member States highlighted the imbalance between the existing State-based legitimacy and the democratic legitimacy which the public expects.

As part of the reform of the institutions, the Treaty of Amsterdam seeks to strike a balance between the institutions which enjoy these two forms of legitimacy, so as to bring about a more democratic distribution of powers and involve Europe's citizens and national parliaments more closely in the decision-making process, one way being by the provision of more information.

A number of changes will be made by the Treaty of Amsterdam, including:

— establishing the co-decision procedure as general practice, while extending the European Parliament's powers in relation to law-making;
— enhancing the legitimacy of the Commission vis-a-vis the European Parliament and the Member States by overhauling the system for the appointment of the Commission and boosting the role of its President.

Intergovernmental Conference (IGC)

This is the term used to describe negotiations between the Member States' governments with a view to amending the treaties. An IGC is of major importance as regards European integration, where changes in the institutional and legal structure — or simply in the content of the treaties — have always been the outcome of intergovernmental conferences (e.g. Single European Act and Treaty on European Union).

There have been six intergovernmental conferences in the history of the European Community, four of them since 1985. The sixth IGC began on 29 March 1996 and ended at the Amsterdam European Council on 16 and 17 June 1997 with the adoption of the Treaty of Amsterdam. It held regular meetings, in principle once a month, at foreign minister level. The preparatory work had been done by a group consisting of a representative of the foreign minister of each Member State and the Member of the Commission with responsibility for institutional matters, with the Council's General Secretariat handling the practical arrangements.

Throughout the Conference, the European Parliament was kept up to date on the state of progress in the discussions and was able to put forward its views on all matters discussed whenever it saw fit.

As the Treaty of Amsterdam did not introduce all the requisite institutional reforms to guarantee the efficiency of the institutions' work after enlargement, the European Council made provision, at the Cologne summit in June 1999, for a seventh IGC in the year 2000. It must reach agreement on the following issues before the end of that year: the size and composition of the Commission, the weighting of votes in the Council and the possible extension of qualified majority voting in the Council.

It should be noted that the negotiations for the accession of new Member States to the European Union take the form of bilateral intergovernmental conferences between the European Union and each of the applicant countries. The intergovernmental conferences on the accession of the Czech Republic, Estonia, Hungary, Poland, Slovenia and Cyprus were formally opened on 30 March 1998. The first ministerial meeting to negotiate with these six applicants took place on 10 November 1998.

Ioannina compromise

The Ioannina compromise takes its name from an informal meeting of foreign ministers in the Greek city of Ioannina on 27 March 1994. Among the decisions taken at the meeting was a Council decision concerning the specific question of qualified majority voting in an enlarged 16-member Community. The decision was later adjusted in the light of Norway's decision not to join. The resulting compromise lays down that if members of the Council representing between 23 votes (the old blocking minority threshold) and 26 votes (the new threshold) express their intention of opposing the taking of a decision by the Council by qualified majority, the Council will do all within its power, within a reasonable space of time, to reach a satisfactory solution that can be adopted by at least 65 votes out of 87.

A declaration annexed to the Treaty of Amsterdam extends this compromise until the next enlargement takes effect.

J

Joint action (CFSP)

This term, which refers to a legal instrument under Title V of the Treaty on European Union, means coordinated action by the Member States whereby resources of all kinds (human resources, know-how, financing, equipment and so on) are mobilised to attain specific objectives fixed by the Council on the base of general guidelines from the European Council.

Joint action (Justice and home affairs)

Joint action was a legal instrument under former Title VI of the EU Treaty that was used between 1993 to 1999. It meant coordinated action by the Member States on behalf of the Union or within the EU framework in cases where, owing to the scale or effects of the envisaged action, the Union's objectives could be attained more effectively by joint action than by the Member States acting individually. It has been abolished by the Treaty of Amsterdam and replaced by 'decisions' and 'framework decisions'.

Joint position (EU Treaty, Title VI)

The joint position was introduced by the Treaty of Maastricht under the heading of cooperation in the fields of justice and home affairs. The Treaty of Amsterdam retains this instrument in the new Title VI of the EU Treaty (police and judicial cooperation in criminal matters).

The joint position is a legal instrument enabling the Council to define the Union's approach on any specific issue. Member States are required to give full effect, both domestically and in foreign policy, to decisions adopted unanimously in meetings of the Council.

Justice and home affairs

Cooperation on justice and home affairs was institutionalised under Title VI of the EU Treaty (also known as the third pillar). The aim of this cooperation was to give practical effect to the principle of the free movement of persons. It covered the following:

— asylum policy;
— rules governing the crossing of the external borders of the Member States;
— immigration policy;
— combating drugs;
— combating international fraud;
— judicial cooperation in civil and criminal matters;
— customs cooperation;
— police cooperation.

Various instruments were created as a means of taking action in this sphere: the joint action, the joint position and the convention. Although significant progress has been made, the overall record of cooperation in this field has been criticised. Consensus has been reached on the need to introduce more effective provisions in order to strengthen the cooperation structures and incorporate into the Community framework the areas mentioned above which are linked to controls on persons (asylum, immigration and crossing of external borders).

The Treaty of Amsterdam has reorganised cooperation in the fields of justice and home affairs, setting as its objective the establishment of an area of freedom, security and justice. Certain sectors have been brought within the Community framework, while at the same time new fields and methods have emerged.

The 'Schengen area', which was formed outside the legal framework of the European Union on the initiative of some of the Member States that wished to advance even further as regards the free movement of persons, will ultimately be incorporated in the EU and EC Treaties.

L
_____

Legal personality of the European Union

The question of the Union's legal status has arisen primarily in connection with its capacity to conclude treaties or accede to agreements or conventions, since the Union, which comprises three separate Communities, each with legal personality (European Community, ECSC and Euratom) and two areas of intergovernmental cooperation, does not have what is known in international law as 'treaty-making powers', that is, the international right to conclude agreements with third countries.

The Treaty of Amsterdam contains no new provisions on the subject, as the Member States failed to reach agreement at the Intergovernmental Conference. Some observers argue that the problem is non-existent and there is nothing to prevent the Union from concluding agreements and asserting its position on the international scene.

Luxembourg compromise

The Luxembourg compromise, reached in January 1966, brought to an end the so-called 'empty chair' crisis, France having refused to take its seat in the Council since July 1965. The compromise was an acknowledgement of the disagreement existing between those who, when a major national interest was at stake, wanted the members of the Council to do their best within a reasonable space of time to find solutions which all sides could adopt without encroaching on their mutual interests, and France, which was in favour of keeping discussions going until unanimous agreement was reached. Subsequently other Member States were to side with the French point of view.

The compromise has not prevented the Council from taking decisions in accordance with the EC Treaty, which provides in many cases for voting by qualified majority. Nor has it hindered the members of the Council from making further efforts to bring points of view closer together before the Council takes a decision.

M

Monetary policy

Monetary policy is covered by Articles 105 to 111 (former Articles 105 to 109) of the EC Treaty. It is fundamental to economic and monetary union (EMU). Decision-making procedures vary according to the topics in hand:

— for the issue of coins by the Member States (Art. 106(2)), the cooperation procedure applies, after consultation of the European Central Bank (ECB);
— for the formulation of exchange-rate policy guidelines (Art. 111(2)), the Council decides by a qualified majority on a recommendation from the ECB or from the Commission after consulting the ECB;
— for the implementing measures referred to in the Statute of the European System of Central Banks (ESCB) (Art. 107(6)) and the limits and conditions under which the ECB is entitled to impose fines (Art. 109(3)), the Council decides by a qualified majority on a recommendation from the ECB and after consulting the European Parliament and the Commission;
— for technical adjustments to the Statute of the ESCB (Art. 107(5)), the Council decides by a qualified majority on a recommendation from the ECB and after consulting the Commission and obtaining the assent of the European Parliament;
— for the exchange rate of the euro against non-Community currencies (Art. 111(1)), the Council decides unanimously on a recommendation from the ECB or the Commission, after consulting the European Parliament.

The institutional provisions (Articles 112–115) and transitional provisions (Articles 116–124) of Title VII of the EC Treaty (economic and monetary policy — former Title VI) have their own special decision-making procedures which are separate from those identified here.

Monitoring the application of Community law

The task of monitoring the application of Community law falls to the European Commission as the guardian of the treaties. It is an expression of the fact that the European Union is based on the rule of law and its purpose is to make sure that the law is observed and actually applied in and by the Member States. In exercising its monitoring function the Commission takes care to safeguard the role which is also assigned to national authorities, particularly the courts, in this area.

Monitoring the application of the law may take the following forms:

— instituting infringement proceedings following complaints or where cases are discovered in the ordinary course of events;
— court action against the other institutions;
— checking whether aid given by the Member States is lawful;
— checking that the principles prohibiting certain types of agreements, decisions and concerted practices and the abuse of a dominant position are observed.

The Commission's annual reports on the application of Community law are an expression of the desire for transparency in dealings not only with complainants but also with citizens and Members of Parliament.

Mr/Ms CFSP

During the intergovernmental conference that led to the Treaty of Amsterdam there was some debate over whether a specific new position should be created under the common foreign and security policy to enable the Union to present itself more visibly and consistently on the international stage by giving it a single, recognisable face and voice. This position, known at the time as 'Mr/Ms CFSP', has now been formally introduced by the Treaty of Amsterdam with the title 'High Representative for the common foreign and security policy'.

'Multi-speed' Europe

'Multi-speed' Europe is the term used to describe the idea of a method of differentiated integration whereby common objectives are pursued by a group of Member States both able and willing to advance, it being implied that the others will follow later.

N

National parliaments

The Conference of European Community Affairs Committees (COSAC) has met every six months since 1989. It consists of representatives of the relevant committees in the national parliaments and of Members of the European Parliament.

With the entry into force of the Maastricht Treaty, the European Union acquired competence in areas which had traditionally been a national preserve, such as justice and home affairs. For this reason, the importance of exchanges between national parliaments and the European Parliament was underlined in a declaration on the role of national parliaments in the European Union. The national governments were also asked to ensure that their parliaments received Commission proposals in good time for possible examination. Providing national parliaments with more information would enable them to be more closely involved in the Community process and to exercise closer democratic control over it.

Under the Treaty of Amsterdam a protocol on the role of national parliaments has been annexed to the EU Treaty, specifying the information that must be sent to national parliaments (White Papers, Green Papers, communications and proposals for legislation). National parliaments have a period of six weeks to discuss a legislative proposal from the date when the Commission makes it available to the European Parliament and the Council up to the date when it is placed on the Council's agenda.

COSAC now also has the power to send the Union institutions any contribution which it deems appropriate and to examine any proposal for a legislative instrument relating to the establishment of the area of freedom, security and justice (which might have a bearing on the rights and freedoms of individuals).

As part of the applicant countries' preparation for accession to the European Union, representatives of the national parliaments of the six first-wave countries (Cyprus, the Czech Republic, Estonia, Hungary, Poland and Slovenia) have been taking part in COSAC's work since accession negotiations began on 30 March 1988.

NATO (North Atlantic Treaty Organisation)

The North Atlantic Treaty Organisation (NATO, or the Atlantic Alliance) was founded in 1949 and has its headquarters in Brussels. It has 19 members: the EU Member States (with the exception of Austria, Finland, Ireland and Sweden), Canada, the United States, Iceland, Norway and Turkey, and, since 12 March 1999, Poland, Hungary and the Czech Republic.

The policy of the Union respects the obligations on certain Member States arising out of NATO membership and is compatible with the common security and defence policy agreed in NATO. The Declaration on Western European Union annexed to the EU Treaty clarifies future relations between NATO and the WEU, which serves as the defence arm of the Union and as a means of strengthening the European pillar of the Atlantic Alliance.

'New-look' NATO

New-look NATO refers to the process of redefining the organisation's role and operation. The key aspects involved are the recognition of a European defence identity, the strengthening of the European component of the transatlantic security system, the new role of the WEU, and the prospect of the eastward enlargement of NATO — initially taking in Hungary, Poland and the Czech Republic — as agreed at the North Atlantic Council meeting in Madrid in July 1997.

This will be accompanied by a deepening of NATO's relations with third countries through partnerships for peace and the North Atlantic Cooperation Council. A major challenge in this connection is that of establishing a sound, stable and sustainable partnership with Russia and Ukraine.

Non-discrimination principle

The aim of this principle is to ensure equality of treatment for individuals irrespective of nationality, sex, racial or ethnic origin, religion or belief, disability, age or sexual orientation.

Article 12 of the EC Treaty (former Article 6) outlaws any discrimination on the grounds of nationality. Under the Treaty of Amsterdam a new Article 13 has been written into the EC Treaty to reinforce the guarantee of non-discrimination laid down in the treaties and extend it to the other cases cited above.

O

OLAF (European Anti-fraud Office)

Since 1 June 1999, the European Anti-fraud Office has been responsible for combating fraud against the European Union budget.

The Office, which was set up under the European Commission Decision of 28 April 1999, replaces the Coordination of Fraud Prevention Unit (UCLAF) in the Commission, set up in 1998 and confined to that one institution. On 6 October 1998 when addressing the European Parliament, Jacques Santer proposed making this department an independent body with extended powers.

The new Office can look into the management and financing of all the Union's institutions and bodies with total operational independence guaranteed by:

— the Director of OLAF: appointed by agreement between Parliament, the Commission and the Council, he is entitled to bring cases before the Court of Justice in order to protect his independence. In addition, he can launch an investigation not only at the request of the institution, body or Member State in question but also on his own initiative;
— OLAF's Supervisory Committee: it is responsible for monitoring investigations and it consists of five well-known independent external figures appointed jointly by Parliament, the Commission and the Council.

The rules governing internal inquiries conducted by OLAF in order to combat fraud, corruption and other unlawful activities carried out to the detriment of the European Communities' financial interests are set out in the Interinstitutional Agreement of 25 May 1999 between Parliament, the Council and the Commission. This Agreement extends the powers of the Office to serious actions which could amount to professional misconduct by officials and other staff and which could lead to disciplinary measures or criminal prosecutions.

Ombudsman

The European Ombudsman is appointed by the European Parliament after each election for the duration of Parliament's term of office. He is empowered to receive complaints from any citizen of the Union or any natural or legal person residing in a Member State concerning instances of maladministration in the activities of the Community institutions or bodies (with the exception of the Court of Justice and the Court of First Instance).

Where the Ombudsman establishes an instance of maladministration he refers the matter to the institution concerned, conducts an investigation, seeks a solution to redress the problem and, if necessary, submits draft recommendations to which the institution is required to reply in the form of a detailed report within three months.

He submits a report to the European Parliament at the end of each annual session.

Opting out

Opting out is an exemption granted to a country that does not wish to join the other Member States in a particular area of Community cooperation as a way of avoiding a general stalemate. The United Kingdom, for instance, asked to be allowed not to take part in the third stage of economic and monetary union (EMU) and similar clauses were agreed with Denmark as regards EMU, defence and European citizenship.

Outermost regions

There are seven 'outermost regions': Guadeloupe, French Guiana, Martinique, Réunion (the four French overseas departments referred to in Article 299(2) of the EC Treaty), the Azores, the Canaries and Madeira. They are the subject of a Declaration annexed to the Treaty.

The Declaration acknowledges that these regions suffer from major structural backwardness and states that, while the provisions of the EC Treaty and secondary legislation automatically apply, it is nonetheless possible to adopt specific measures to assist them as long as there is a real objective need for such measures to promote their economic and social development.

Article 299(2) has been amended by the Treaty of Amsterdam to enable the Council, acting by a qualified majority, to adopt specific decisions laying down conditions for applying the Treaty, including the common policies, to the outermost regions. In so doing, the Council has to ensure that the integrity and coherence of the Community legal order is not undermined.

Own resources

Own resources are the tax revenue allocated to the European Union to finance its expenditure, which must not exceed the current ceiling of 1.27 % of Community GNP. Originally, the Community budget depended on the Member States' financial contributions. However, a decision was adopted on 21 April 1970 giving it financial autonomy, and since 1 January 1978, the Community budget has been entirely financed by own resources. These are currently made up of four elements:

— agricultural duties and the sugar and isoglucose levies; these consist mainly of the agricultural duties and, under the common organisation of the sugar markets, production and storage levies;
— customs duties: these come from the application of the common customs tariff to imports from third countries;
— the VAT resource: this comes from the application of a flat rate to the VAT base of each Member State (in 1999, this flat rate will be 1 %, to be collected on a base which may not exceed 50 % of GNP);
— the 'fourth resource': introduced in 1988, this is a so-called additional resource, because it is set according to the other three sources of budget revenue. It is based on GNP and the application of a rate, set under the budget procedure, to the total GNP of all the Member States.

In 1999, the forecast revenue of the European Union came to EUR 86 million, of which about 48.1 % came from the GNP resource, 35.2 % from the VAT resource, 13.8 % from customs duties and 2.2 % from agricultural levies.

P

Parliamentary committees

Various committees have been set up within the European Parliament to organise its work. The members of each committee are elected at the beginning of and half-way through each parliamentary term, according to their political affiliation and their expertise.

Parliament's Rules of Procedure specify that the Members of Parliament set the number of committees and determine their powers. At present there are 17 specialised permanent committees in which the Commission's proposals are discussed. Parliament can also set up sub-committees, temporary committees and committees of inquiry if it considers it necessary. Two committees of inquiry have been set up so far: on the Community transit procedure in 1996 and on the bovine spongiform encephalopathy (BSE) epidemic in 1997.

The main task of the permanent committees is to debate proposals for new legislation put forward by the European Commission and to draw up own-initiative reports. For any proposal for legislation or other initiative, a rapporteur is nominated according to an agreement between the political groups which make up Parliament. His or her report is discussed, amended and voted on within the parliamentary committee and then transmitted to the plenary assembly, which meets once a month in Strasbourg, and which debates and votes on the basis of this report.

As preparation for Parliament's vote of approval of the European Commission, the parliamentary committees also hear the proposed Members of the Commission in their specialised areas.

Petersberg Declaration (Petersberg tasks)

The Petersberg Declaration of 19 June 1992 is a pivotal element in the determination to develop the Western European Union (WEU) as the defence arm of the EU and as a means of strengthening the European pillar of the Atlantic Alliance (NATO). The three parts of the declaration define the guidelines for the future development of the WEU.

WEU Member States declare their readiness to make available military units from the whole spectrum of their conventional armed forces for military tasks conducted under the authority of WEU. The different types of military tasks which WEU might undertake were defined: apart from contributing to the common defence in accordance with Article 5 of the Washington Treaty and Article V of the modified Brussels Treaty, military units of WEU Member States could be employed for:

— humanitarian and rescue tasks;
— peacekeeping tasks;
— tasks of combat forces in crisis management, including peacemaking.

The Treaty of Amsterdam has specifically incorporated these 'Petersberg tasks' in the new Article 17 of the EU Treaty.

The Petersberg Declaration also states that WEU is prepared to support, on a case-by-case basis and in accordance with its own procedures, the effective implementation of conflict-prevention and crisis-management measures, including peacekeeping activities of the CSCE (now OSCE) or the United Nations Security Council.

At the same time, the Declaration supports a solid transatlantic partnership and stresses the importance of implementing the Declaration on WEU (No 30) annexed to the Maastricht Treaty. The third part of the Declaration relates to the enlargement of the WEU: in it the Member States define the rights and obligations of other European States belonging to the European Union and the Atlantic Alliance as future members, observers or associate members.

Petitions

The right of petition is the right which every citizen of the European Union enjoys, individually or in association with other citizens, to submit a request to the European Parliament or to table a grievance before it on any subject which falls within the spheres of activity of the Community and concerns him or her directly (Articles 21 and 194 of the EC Treaty, formerly Articles 8d and 138d).

Parliament's Committee on Petitions considers whether such requests are admissible. Where it sees fit, it may put a question to the Ombudsman. When drawing up an opinion on a petition deemed to be admissible, it may ask the European Commission to provide it with documents or information.

The Treaty of Amsterdam added a new paragraph to Article 21, stating that every citizen of the Union may write to any of the institutions, including the Committee of the Regions and the Economic and Social Committee, and to the Ombudsman in any of the official Union languages (including Irish) and receive an answer written in the same language.

Phare

The Phare programme was launched in 1989 following the collapse of the communist regimes in central and eastern Europe. It is intended to help these countries reconstruct their economies. Originally, it affected only Poland and Hungary but it has gradually been extended to cover 13 central and eastern European countries today (Albania, Bosnia-Herzegovina, Bulgaria, the Czech Republic, Estonia, FYROM, Hungary, Latvia, Lithuania, Poland, Romania, Slovakia and Slovenia).

For the period 1995–99, funding under Phare totalled roughly EUR 6.7 billion and covered 15 sectors, the main five of which were:

— infrastructure (energy, transport, telecommunication);
— development of the private sector and assistance for businesses;
— education, training and research;
— environmental protection and nuclear safety;
— agricultural restructuring.

At the same time, Phare is the main financial instrument for the pre-accession strategy for the 10 central and eastern European countries (CEECs) which have applied for membership of the European Union. Since 1994, Phare's tasks have been adapted to the priorities and needs of each CEEC.

The revamped Phare programme with a budget of over EUR 10 billion for the period 2000–06 now has two specific priorities, namely:

— institution building
— financing investments.

Following the proposals put forward by the Commission in its Agenda 2000 communication in July 1997, new forms of pre-accession aid have been added to that already provided by Phare. These are:

— structural measures to bring the level of environmental protection and of transport infrastructure development in the applicant countries closer to that of the European Union (ISPA)
— aid to agriculture (Sapard).

Pillars of the European Union

In Community parlance people often refer to the three pillars of the EU Treaty. These are:

— the Community dimension, comprising the arrangements set out in the EC, ECSC and Euratom Treaties, i.e. Union citizenship, Community policies, economic and monetary union, etc. (first pillar);
— the common foreign and security policy, which comes under Title V of the EU Treaty (second pillar);
— police and judicial cooperation in criminal matters, which comes under Title VI of the EU Treaty (third pillar).

The Treaty of Amsterdam has transferred some of the fields covered by the old third pillar to the first pillar (free movement of persons).

Planning and Early Warning Unit

The idea of setting up a Planning and Early Warning Unit under the common foreign and security policy stems from the belief that if the CFSP is to be effective, it will require earlier and more far-reaching analysis of external developments in the long, medium and short term. The decisions taken under the CFSP must therefore be underpinned by more reliable briefings, which are available to all the Member States of the Union.

In a declaration to the Final Act, the Intergovernmental Conference agreed to set up a Planning and Early Warning Unit in the General Secretariat of the Council, placed under the responsibility of its Secretary-General. The staff of the Unit are drawn from the General Secretariat of the Council, the Member States, the Commission and the Western European Union (WEU).

Police and judicial cooperation in criminal matters

Title VI of the EU Treaty (or the third pillar) has been completely transformed by the Treaty of Amsterdam with the creation of an area of freedom, security and justice. Previously known under the heading 'Justice and home affairs', it now covers only 'police and judicial cooperation in criminal matters', the objective being to prevent and combat the following problems:

— racism and xenophobia;
— terrorism;
— trafficking in human beings and crimes against children;
— drug trafficking;
— arms trafficking;
— corruption and fraud.

The new Title provides for closer cooperation between police forces, customs and judicial authorities, both directly and through the European Police Office (Europol), and, where necessary, the alignment of criminal law in the Member States.

The Council will continue to play the leading role under this pillar, but some of the instruments at its disposal have changed. The common position and the convention remain, but joint action has been replaced by two new instruments: decisions and framework decisions.

Furthermore, the Schengen *acquis* developed by some of the Member States in an intergovernmental framework, which also covers police and judicial cooperation, is due to be incorporated into the European Union and Community framework in the near future.

Political agenda of the European Union

The Madrid European Council (15–16 December 1995) described the European Union's agenda for the end of the century as laying the foundations for the Europe of the future, a large community enjoying the benefits of freedom, prosperity and stability. In practical terms this means:

— adjusting the Treaty on European Union;
— making the transition to a single currency in line with the agreed timetable and conditions;
— preparing for and carrying out the enlargement negotiations;
— adopting the financial perspective for the period beyond 31 December 1999;
— contributing to establishing the new European security architecture;
— actively continuing the policy of dialogue, cooperation and association already under way with the Union's neighbouring countries, and in particular with Russia, Ukraine, Turkey and the Mediterranean countries.

Political Committee

The Political Committee consists of political directors from the Member States' foreign ministries. It monitors the international situation in fields covered by the common foreign and security policy and helps determine policy by issuing opinions for the Council. It also supervises the implementation of agreed policies, without prejudice to the powers of the presidency and the Commission.

Pre-accession aid

Enormous investment is required if the applicant countries are to adapt their standards, especially their industrial and environmental norms, in order to be able to comply with Community legislation when they join the Union. The pre-accession aid planned for the period 2000–06 for the countries of central and eastern Europe is a key element of the European Union's strategy towards the applicants and involves two main components:

— the Phare programme finances the projects needed to adapt the applicant countries' administrative and legal systems and to develop their infrastructure (EUR 10.5 billion);
— two assistance funds are being set up to manage additional aid for agriculture (Sapard — EUR 3.5 billion) and infrastructure, especially in the fields of the environment and transport (EUR 7 billion). The fund devoted to infrastructure development is the 'structural pre-accession instrument', which will play the same role for the applicant countries as the Cohesion Fund does for Spain, Portugal, Greece and Ireland.

The accession partnership concluded in 1998 with each of the 10 applicant countries of central and eastern Europe constitutes the main thrust of the pre-accession strategy and serves as the channel for the various types of aid.

Cyprus is not covered by the Phare programme and therefore comes under different arrangements. A financial protocol awarded it total assistance of EUR 72 million for the period 1996–2000.

Pre-accession pact on organised crime

In preparation for the enlargement of the European Union, on 28 May 1998 the ministers for justice and home affairs of the Member States and the applicant countries adopted a 'pre-accession pact on organised crime' with the aim of:

— associating the applicant countries with the European Union's priority actions;
— helping the applicant countries to adopt the *acquis communautaire* in justice and home affairs;
— setting up joint projects against crime for which technical or financial assistance from the Union would be helpful.

The applicant countries undertook to rapidly adopt a number of international conventions, particularly regarding extradition (1957 European Convention), drug trafficking (UN Convention) and terrorism (1977 European Convention). Agreements with Europol are planned, in order to promote exchanges and information and to define priorities for the action undertaken by the European Union and its partners.

Pre-accession strategy

In 1989, the European Commission put in place a financial assistance programme intended to facilitate the economic and political transition of the countries of central and eastern Europe (Phare programme). In 1991, the first association agreements (so-called Europe Agreements) were signed by the European Community and the countries of central and eastern Europe. Interim agreements were put in place in order to immediately start to set up a free trade area. Although restrictions remained for agricultural and iron and steel products, the free movement of goods is now a reality for 26 European countries.

On the basis of the Europe Agreements, in 1993 the Commission proposed the organisation of a 'structured dialogue' between the associated countries and the institutions of the Union in the form of meetings where the different partners could consult each other.

In December 1994, the Essen European Council adopted a pre-accession strategy based on:

— deepening relations between the associated countries and the institutions of the Union (strengthening the structured dialogue at the level of Parliament and the government);
— development of Europe Agreements;
— adaptation of the financial assistance provided by Phare;
— preparation for integration into the internal market;

Starting from the Madrid European Council (December 1995), questions began to be raised about the repercussions of enlargement on Community policies, particularly on the common agricultural policy, the structural policies and the Union's financial perspective after 1999. 'Agenda 2000', presented by the Commission in July 1997, proposed reforms relating to these three crucial subjects for the future of the European Union.

In parallel with this debate, new instruments were created to support the applicant countries in their preparation for accession, in both financial and legislative terms. In 1998, accession partnerships for each of the 10 countries of central and eastern Europe were launched.

For Cyprus, a special pre-accession strategy was put in place:

— participation in targeted action in order to strengthen its administrative and institutional capacity and to act in the field of justice and home affairs;
— participation in certain programmes and Community agencies (like all the applicant countries);
— use of the TAIEX technical assistance office to help it to adapt its legislation to Community rules.

Presidency of the Union (rotation of the Presidency)

The Presidency of the Union is held in turn on a six-monthly basis by each Member State. A stint in the Presidency is a duty and a contribution that each Member State makes to the proper functioning of the Community institutions. At present, a Member State holds the Presidency every seven and a half years.

President of the European Commission

The Treaty of Amsterdam strengthens the role and position of the Commission President. The governments of the Member States designate the person they intend to appoint as President by common accord — a choice which then has to be approved by the European Parliament.

The governments then designate the persons they intend to appoint as Members of the Commission, in agreement with the new President. The President lays down the broad policy lines to be followed by the Commission in its work. He also decides on the allocation of portfolios among the Commissioners and any reshuffling of portfolios during the Commission's term of office.

In a declaration on the organisation and functioning of the Commission annexed to the EC Treaty, the Intergovernmental Conference recommended that, for the sake of consistency, responsibility for external relations be assigned to a Vice-President (at present it is divided between five individuals).

Public health

Public health is covered by Article 152 of the EC Treaty (former Article 129), which was introduced by the Treaty of Maastricht. This article states that Community action is to focus on the prevention of illnesses, including drug addiction, by promoting research into their causes and their transmission, as well as health information and education. The Treaty of Amsterdam reinforces these objectives by requiring that the definition and implementation of all Community policies and activities ensures a high level of human health protection.

Under Article 152 action towards these ends may involve Community measures, complementing action by the Member States. But the main approach should be to encourage cooperation between the Member States, in line with the subsidiarity principle.

The institutional arrangements are that the Council adopts incentive actions on the basis of the co-decision procedure, while recommendations are adopted by qualified majority on a Commission proposal. The Treaty of Amsterdam extends the scope of actions covered by the co-decision procedure to include measures setting high standards of quality and safety of organs and substances of human origin, as well as measures in the veterinary and phytosanitary fields.

Public service

The concept of public service is a twofold one: it embraces both bodies providing services and the general-interest services they provide. Public-service obligations may be imposed by the public authorities on the body providing a service (airlines, road or rail carriers, energy producers and so on), either nationally or regionally. Incidentally, the concept of the public service and the concept of the public sector (including the civil service) are often, wrongly, confused; they differ in terms of function, status, ownership and 'clientele'.

Public service charter

The idea behind a public service charter is that there should be an instrument setting out the basic rights and principles governing the provision of services to users. Such principles would include:

— continuity of service;
— quality;
— security of supply;
— equal access;
— affordable prices;
— social, cultural and environmental acceptability.

Q

Qualified majority

A qualified majority is the number of votes required in the Council for a decision to be adopted when issues are being debated on the basis of Article 205(2) of the EC Treaty (former Article 148(2)). The threshold for the qualified majority is set at 62 votes out of 87 (71 %). The votes are weighted as follows: France, Germany, Italy and United Kingdom 10 votes each; Spain 8 votes; Belgium, Greece, the Netherlands and Portugal 5 votes each; Austria and Sweden 4 votes each; Denmark, Ireland and Finland 3 votes each; Luxembourg 2 votes.

Recasting of legislation

The recasting of legislation means the adoption, when an amendment is made to a basic instrument, of a new legal instrument which incorporates the said amendment into the basic instrument, but repeals and replaces the latter. Unlike formal consolidation, it involves changes of substance. It also gives a comprehensive overview of an area of legislation. The new legal instrument is published in the Official Journal (L series).

Reflection Group for the 1996 IGC (Westendorp Group)

The task of the Reflection Group, which was set up by the European Council held in Corfu on 24 and 25 June 1994, was to prepare the ground for the 1996 Intergovernmental Conference (IGC) by proposing possible ways of responding to the internal and external challenges facing the Union.

It comprised representatives of the Member States' foreign ministers, of the European Parliament (Elmar Brok, a German member of the EPP, and Elisabeth Guigou, a French member of the PES) and of the Member of the Commission with responsibility for institutional matters, Marcelino Oreja. It was chaired by Carlos Westendorp, who was appointed by the Spanish Government.

The Group met for discussion from June to December 1995, and each institution contributed to its work by drawing up a preliminary report on the functioning of the Treaty on European Union. The conclusions reached by the Group were passed on to the Madrid European Council (15 and 16 December 1995) and formed a working basis for the Intergovernmental Conference.

Reinforced qualified majority

The idea of a reinforced qualified majority stems from the conviction shared by several Member States and the European Commission that if the unanimity requirement is maintained in an enlarged Union it will all too often result in stalemate. Unanimity might therefore be replaced in certain cases by a reinforced qualified majority, larger than the 71 % of the votes generally required for majority voting. Several proposals have been put forward as to the areas where such a majority would apply and the exact level of the threshold.

This option might be discussed at the next intergovernmental conference, which will carry out a comprehensive review of the Treaty provisions on the composition and functioning of the institutions. A protocol annexed to the EU Treaty by the Treaty of Amsterdam requires such a conference to be convened at least one year before the number of members of the European Union exceeds 20.

Research and development

European research and development policy is based on provisions in the three founding treaties (ECSC, Euratom and Title XVIII of the EC Treaty). The Single European Act introduced the concept of technology into Community law and the EU Treaty then developed the Community's objectives in this field. Supporting the competitiveness of European industry and promoting research to help it face technological challenges are the Community's priorities.

The coordination of initiatives in research and development within the Community is based on various instruments:

— the framework programme for research and technological development. This multi-annual programme, set up in 1984, coordinates more specific programmes dedicated to fields as varied as information and communication technologies, the environment, biology, energy (including nuclear), transport and mobility of researchers. The fifth framework programme (1998–2002) has been allocated more than EUR 14.9 billion to achieve its objectives, including promotion of a user-friendly information society and access to research for small businesses;
— the Joint Research Centre (JRC) and the Euratom Supply Agency. The JRC is made up of eight research institutes set up across the European Community to meet the specific needs of the Commission. It is at the forefront of research in nuclear energy (especially security) and has diversified into sectors such as materials, the environment, and industrial risks;
— COST, which was set up in 1971, covers 25 countries: the 15 Member States of the European Union plus Iceland, Norway, Switzerland, Croatia, the Czech Republic, Hungary, Poland, Slovakia, Slovenia and Turkey. The aim of this European cooperation programme is to coordinate national research priorities in Europe;
— Eureka is an intergovernmental organisation of 26 countries including the Member States of the European Union, Russia, Switzerland and Turkey. It was set up in 1985 and aims to support partnerships between businesses and research institutes, especially in advanced technology sectors.

The multiannual framework programme is adopted under the co-decision procedure. Unanimity in the Council is no longer required following the entry into force of the Treaty of Amsterdam. The specific programmes are always adopted by the Council by a qualified majority on a Commission proposal, after consulting the European Parliament and the Economic and Social Committee.

Right of initiative

So that it can play its role as guardian of the treaties and defender of the general interest the Commission has been given a right of initiative which empowers and requires it to make proposals on the matters contained in the Treaty, either because the Treaty expressly so provides or because the Commission considers it necessary.

— This power of initiative is exclusive in respect of Community matters, the principle being that the Council takes decisions only 'on a proposal from the Commission', so that there is a coherent framework for all initiatives.
— Under the common foreign and security policy the Commission may make proposals, as may the Member States. On the other hand it has no such right in certain matters relating to justice and home affairs.

The Council and the European Parliament may also ask the Commission to put forward a proposal if they consider it necessary.

The right of initiative is regarded as a basic element in the institutional balance of the Community.

The Treaty of Amsterdam has extended the Commission's right of initiative to the new policies (health and employment), to matters relating to the free movement of persons, and to the third pillar. In the case of the third pillar, the Commission shares the right of initiative with the Member States.

Rural development

Rural development is closely linked to the common agricultural policy and measures to support employment. Accordingly, support measures in this sector have been traditionally based on different legal instruments pursuing different objectives.

In order to make it fully coherent, the reform of the common agricultural policy in 1999 under Agenda 2000, was accompanied by the strengthening of rural development measures, which were arranged in a single regulation.

This instrument establishes an integrated policy of sustainable rural development which ensures greater coherence between rural development and the prices and markets policy of the common agricultural policy, and promotes all aspects of rural development by encouraging all the local players to become involved.

Rural development has thus become the second pillar of the agricultural policy. With its links to agricultural activities and conversion, it is concerned in particular with:

— modernisation of farms;
— safety and quality of food products;
— fair and stable incomes for farmers;
— environmental challenges;
— supplementary or alternative job-creating activities, in a bid to halt the drift from the country and to strengthen the economic and social fabric of rural areas;
— improvement of living and working conditions, and promotion of equal opportunities.

The rural development measures designed to achieve these objectives have been divided into two categories:

— flanking measures in the 1992 CAP reform: early retirement, agro-environmental measures, afforestation and the scheme for less-favoured areas;
— measures to modernise and diversify farms: investment in farms, start-up schemes for young farmers, training, support for investments in processing and marketing plants, supplementary aid for forestry, promoting and restructuring agriculture.

S

Schengen (Agreement and Convention)

By the agreement signed at Schengen on 14 June 1985, Belgium, Germany, France, Luxembourg and the Netherlands agreed that they would gradually remove their common frontier controls and introduce freedom of movement for all individuals who were nationals of the signatory Member States, other Member States or third countries.

The Schengen Convention was signed by the same five States on 19 June 1990. It lays down the arrangements and guarantees for implementing freedom of movement. It amends the relevant national laws and is subject to parliamentary ratification. Italy (1990), Spain and Portugal (1991), Greece (1992), Austria (1995), Sweden, Finland and Denmark (1996) have since joined the list of signatories, while Iceland and Norway are also parties to the convention.

The agreement and the convention, together with the declarations and decisions adopted by the Schengen Executive Committee, make up what is known as the Schengen *acquis*. When the Treaty of Amsterdam was being drafted, it was decided to incorporate this *acquis* into the European Union from 1 May 1999 onwards, since it relates to one of the main objectives of the single market, i.e. the free movement of persons.

For that purpose, the Council of Ministers first identified the measures which formed the real 'Schengen *acquis*'. Subsequently, in order to give them a legal basis, it established whether they came under the new Title IV (Visas, asylum, immigration and other policies related to the free movement of persons) of the Treaty establishing the European Communities or Title VI (Provisions on police and judicial cooperation in criminal matters) of the Treaty on European Union.

The legal incorporation of Schengen into the European Union was accompanied by integration of the institutions. The Council took over the Schengen Executive Committee and the Council's General Secretariat took over the Schengen Secretariat.

An agreement was signed on 18 May 1999, between the European Union and Iceland and Norway, countries outside the Community which are party to Schengen. It associates them with the implementation and development of the Schengen *acquis*, and sets out how they are to participate in the free movement area in the European Union.

It is still possible for a smaller number of Member States to pursue reinforced cooperation between them if they so desire.

Screening

In May 1995 the White Paper on preparing the countries of central and eastern Europe for integration into the Union's single market drew up an initial table of the Community legislation that they will have to incorporate into their own law before joining the European Union. On 30 March 1998, the negotiations began for the accession of the applicant countries designated by the Luxembourg European Council in December 1997. On 3 April 1998, analysis of the Community *acquis* began.

This first stage consists of evaluating the compatibility of each applicant country's legislation with Community rules. This screening process is carried out jointly by the Commission and each of the applicant countries and will last until at least June 1999. Sector by sector, it allows a road map to be drawn up for each applicant indicating which legislative instruments must be adopted or amended so that the future member will be able to adhere to Community legislation as soon as possible after accession. A technical assistance office, TAIEX, is responsible for carrying out the survey of Community legislation (the Community *acquis*) and the applicant countries' measures incorporating these principles.

The screening exercise is essential because it will serve as a basis for bilateral negotiations between the European Union and each of the applicant countries.

Services of general economic interest

Services of general economic interest are commercial services of general economic utility, on which the public authorities therefore impose specific public-service obligations (Article 86 of the EC Treaty, formerly Article 90). Transport, energy and communications services are prime examples.

A new Article 16 has been written into the EC Treaty by the Treaty of Amsterdam, acknowledging the place occupied by services of general economic interest in the shared values of the Union and their role in promoting social and territorial cohesion. Article 16 also states that such services must operate on the basis of principles and conditions which enable them to fulfil their functions.

Simplification of legislation

Simplifying legislation means weeding out the superfluous by rigorously applying the tests of whether it is necessary and proportionate. The exercise mainly involves the recasting and formal or informal consolidation of legislation.

This concept has grown in importance since the White Paper on the completion of the single market and was explicitly put forward by the Edinburgh European Council in 1992. Over the past decade a concentrated effort has been made to establish a market guaranteeing the four freedoms, but this has meant a wealth of European legislation. Simplifying this mass of law has now become a priority in order to ensure that Community action is transparent and effective. A pilot programme (Simpler legislation for the internal market — SLIM) covering four specific areas was launched in May 1996 and could be extended to other areas.

A declaration on the quality of the drafting of Community legislation is attached to the Final Act of the Intergovernmental Conference (1997). It recommends that the European Parliament, the Council and the Commission lay down guidelines for improving the form of legislation and calls on the institutions to make a determined effort to speed up the official consolidation of legislative texts.

Single institutional framework

The single institutional framework is the practical expression of the principle that there is only one set of institutions. It presupposes that Member States wishing to integrate and cooperate still further will agree to act through shared institutions. It also requires the other non-participating Member States to accept that shared institutions can be used for such operations to knit the Union closer together without involving all the Member States.

Social Charter

All the Member States except the United Kingdom adopted the Charter of the Fundamental Social Rights of Workers, commonly known as the Social Charter, in 1989 in the form of a declaration. It is seen as a political instrument containing 'moral obligations' whose object is to guarantee that certain social rights are respected in the countries concerned. These primarily relate to the labour market, vocational training, equal opportunities and the working environment. It also contains an explicit request to the Commission to put forward proposals for translating the content of the Social Charter into legislation. The Social Charter has been followed up by social action programmes.

Social dialogue

Social dialogue is the term used to describe a joint consultation procedure involving the social partners at European level (UNICE, CEEP, ESC). It involves discussion, joint action and sometimes negotiations between the European social partners, and discussions between the social partners and the Union institutions.

It was started by the European Commission in 1985, and ever since the Single European Act the Treaty has formally required the Commission to develop the dialogue (Article 139, formerly Article 118b). So far the outcome has been 15 joint opinions on (among other things) economic growth, the introduction of new technology, education, and vocational training. Social dialogue may also lead to contractual relationships, including agreements, the implementation of which is subject to a decision by the Council on a proposal from the Commission. There have been two agreements of this type between employers and labour to date — on parental leave and on part-time working.

Besides this ongoing dialogue between the two sides of industry, the Commission organised the first European Forum on social policy in March 1996, which brought together representatives of voluntary organisations, non-governmental organisations, trade unions, employers' organisations, the European Union institutions and the Member States.

— the European Regional Development Fund (ERDF), set up in 1975;
— the Financial Instrument for Fisheries Guidance (FIFG), created in 1993.

From 1994 to 1999, Structural Fund assistance was provided, subject to the principles of concentration, partnership, additionality and planning, for 7 objectives and 13 initiatives.

In order to improve the effectiveness of Community action during the period 2000–06, the Commission communication 'Agenda 2000', published in July 1997, proposed that the structural policy be reformed. This reform increased the concentration of aid and simplified its operation by reducing the number of objectives to three:

— development and structural adjustment of the regions whose development is lagging behind and whose per capita GNP is less than 75 % of the European Union average (Objective 1: it receives 70 % of the Structural Funds);
— the economic and social conversion of areas with structural difficulties (Objective 2: this covers areas with economic diversification problems, i.e. areas undergoing economic change, rural areas in decline, areas in crisis dependent on fishing and urban areas in difficulty);
— the development of human resources outside the regions eligible for Objective 1 (Objective 3: this is the reference framework for all the measures taken under the new title on employment in the Amsterdam Treaty and the European employment strategy).

Community initiatives have been reduced to four:

— Interreg, whose objective is to stimulate cross-border, transnational and inter-regional cooperation;
— Leader, which aims to encourage rural development through initiatives by local action groups;
— Equal, which provides for the development of new practices to fight against discrimination and inequalities of every kind in access to the labour market;
— Urban, which encourages economic and social revitalisation of cities and suburbs in crisis.

Economic and monetary union has also highlighted the existence of serious economic and social disparities between the Member States of the European Union. A Cohesion Fund was set up in 1993 to strengthen the structural policy. This is intended for those countries with a per capita GNP of less than 90 % of the Community average, i.e. Greece, Spain, Ireland and Portugal. The aim of the Cohesion Fund is to grant funds for environment and transport infrastructure projects.

Subsidiarity

The subsidiarity principle is intended to ensure that decisions are taken as closely as possible to the citizen and that constant checks are made as to whether action at Community level is justified in the light of the possibilities available at national, regional or local level. Specifically, it is the principle whereby the Union does not take action (except in the areas which fall within its exclusive competence) unless it is more effective than action taken at national, regional or local level. It is closely bound up with the principles of proportionality and necessity, which require that any action by the Union should not go beyond what is necessary to achieve the objectives of the Treaty.

The Edinburgh European Council of December 1992 defined the basic principles underlying subsidiarity and laid down guidelines for interpreting Article 5 (former Article 3b), which enshrines subsidiarity in the EU Treaty. Its conclusions were set out in a declaration that still serves as the cornerstone of the subsidiarity principle. The Treaty of Amsterdam has taken up the overall approach that follows from this declaration in a protocol on the application of the principles of subsidiarity and proportionality annexed to the EC Treaty.

Each year the European Commission produces a report ('Better lawmaking') for the European Council and the European Parliament which is devoted mainly to the application of the subsidiarity principle.

Suspension clause

The suspension clause was written into the EU Treaty (Article 7) by the Treaty of Amsterdam.

Under this clause, some of a Member State's rights (e.g. its voting rights in the Council) may be suspended if it breaches the principles on which the Union is founded (liberty, democracy, respect for human rights and fundamental freedoms, and the rule of law). Its obligations, however, would still be binding.

Sustainable development

The concept of sustainable development refers to a form of economic growth which satisfies society's needs in terms of well-being in the short, medium and — above all — long terms. It is founded on the assumption that development must meet today's needs without jeopardising the prospects of future generations. In practical terms, it means creating the conditions for long-term economic development with due respect for the environment. The Copenhagen world summit for sustainable development (March 1995) stressed the need to combat social exclusion and protect public health.

The Treaty of Amsterdam wrote an explicit reference to sustainable development into the recitals of the EU Treaty.

T

TAIEX

TAIEX, the technical assistance exchange office, was created in response to a proposal in the White Paper on the preparation of the associated countries of central and eastern Europe for integration into the Union's internal market (May 1995). This service, managed by the European Commission, was originally intended to assist and inform the countries of central and eastern Europe on single market legislation so as to facilitate its implementation. It now deals with all the applicant countries, since the decision by the Luxembourg European Council in December 1997.

TAIEX deals with the public administrations in the applicant countries and the Member States. It provides the legal texts of the Community *acquis* and organises training seminars and visits by experts to countries which so request. It has a key role in the process of assessing whether the legislation of the applicant countries conforms with Community legislation (screening).

Although the office is independent of the Phare programme, their activities are connected, as Phare can finance certain activities offered by TAIEX.

Taxation

Despite the introduction of a single market and economic and monetary union, there is still no genuine Community policy on taxation. Specific provisions are laid down in Articles 90 to 93 of the EC Treaty (former Articles 95 to 99), but the decision-making procedure for taxation requires a unanimous vote in the Council. Up to now this has acted as a brake on the adoption of common rules for direct and indirect taxation.

Border controls on VAT were abolished with the introduction of the single market in 1993. Today, products are taxed in the country of purchase but eventually, when the final VAT system has been decided by the Council, they will be taxed in the country of origin. Furthermore, VAT and excise rates have been brought into closer alignment in the different Member States.

The adoption of the single currency is making it increasingly urgent to establish truly common rates of VAT and common rules for corporate taxation in the European Union. A code of conduct on business taxation was adopted by the Council in December 1997. Various Commission proposals are currently being scrutinised by the Council, notably on relations between associated companies, taxation of cross-border savings and a common VAT system.

Telecommunications

With the prospect of the internal market being completed, telecommunications liberalisation emerged as a priority for the European Community in 1987 (Green Paper on the development of the common market for telecommunications services and equipment). In 1988, a directive opened the telecommunications terminals markets up to competition. This was supplemented in 1994 by provisions on satellite equipment.

In the second phase of this development, a directive adopted in 1990 liberalised telecommunications services other than voice telephony. It was extended in 1994 to satellite communications and broadcasting services and then, in 1996, to cable television networks and mobile communications. At the same time, an open telecommunications infrastructure and services network (ONP) was put in place from 1990. The adoption of common rules allowed the conditions of access to the market for new operators to be harmonised. Also in 1990, a directive liberalised procedures for the award of contracts in water, energy and telecommunications.

In 1993, the Council decided to fully liberalise voice telephony services by 1 January 1998. Luxembourg has two extra years because of the size of its network. An extension was given to Spain, Ireland, Greece and Portugal until 2003. At the same time, a Commission communication defined the concept of universal service, detailing the provision and quality of the service, the charging principles and the dispute settlement procedures.

The concept of the 'information society', with its attendant promise of economic growth and job creation, started to take hold from 1994. The general liberalisation of telecommunications structures was pushed forward from this time to allow multimedia development. In 1995, it was decided that it should proceed under the same conditions as the liberalisation of voice telephony services.

In order to facilitate the creation of a genuine European telecommunications market, various initiatives were adopted on the harmonisation of mobile (single European GSM standard) and satellite communications standards, and the integrated services digital network (ISDN). The European Community also finances research programmes in information technologies and the creation of trans-European telecommunications networks, thanks to the European Regional Development Fund and the European Investment Bank.

Title V of the EU Treaty (CFSP)

Title V of the EU Treaty, also known as the second pillar, contains the provisions establishing a common foreign and security policy. It comprises Articles 11 to 28.

Title VI of the EU Treaty

Introduced by the Treaty of Maastricht, Title VI of the EU Treaty — or the third pillar — contained provisions establishing cooperation on justice and home affairs.

The Treaty of Amsterdam has transferred a large number of fields which used to come under Title VI to a new Title IV of the EC Treaty ('Visas, asylum, immigration and other policies related to free movement of persons'). Police and judicial cooperation in criminal matters remains under Title VI of the EU Treaty, which now comprises 14 articles (Articles 29 to 42).

Title IV of the EC Treaty and Title VI of the EU Treaty now constitute the legal bases for an area of freedom, security and justice.

Transparency

The term 'transparency' is frequently used in the language of the institutions to mean openness in the working of the Community institutions. It is linked to a variety of demands for broader public access to information and EU documents and more easily readable instruments (simplification of the treaties, consolidation and better drafting of legislation).

Complaints regarding a lack of transparency tend to reflect a general feeling that the European institutions are remote and secretive and that decision-making procedures are difficult for the ordinary European citizen to understand.

The Treaty of Amsterdam has inserted a new Article 255 on transparency in the EC Treaty. This gives all citizens of the European Union, plus all natural or legal persons residing or having their registered offices in a Member State, the right of access to European Parliament, Council and Commission documents. The general principles and any restrictions on access to such documents (on grounds of public or private interest) have to be determined by the Council, acting with Parliament under the co-decision procedure, within two years after the entry into force of the new Treaty. All three institutions are required to incorporate special provisions on access to their documents in their rules of procedure.

Transparency of Council proceedings

In the debate concerning the transparency of the Council's proceedings, attention is focused on two main points:

— public access to the Council's proceedings;
— public access to Council minutes and the attached statements giving details of the voting.

Since amending its Rules of Procedure on 6 December 1993, the Council has pursued the following policy: as a general rule, its deliberations remain secret but it holds some open debates (e.g. on the Presidency's six-monthly work programme). On the question of public access and details of the votes cast by Member States, the Council adopted (on 2 October 1995) a Code of Conduct which enables the public to gain access whenever the Council is acting in its legislative role. The practical arrangements for such access were laid down by the Permanent Representatives Committee on 8 November, in a report concerning the internal procedure to be followed.

The Treaty of Amsterdam has formally enshrined the principles governing access to documents in Article 207 of the EC Treaty. This means that the results and explanations of Council votes and statements entered in the minutes are now available to the general public.

Treaty of Amsterdam

The Treaty of Amsterdam is the result of the Intergovernmental Conference launched at the Turin European Council on 29 March 1996. It was adopted at the Amsterdam European Council on 16 and 17 June 1997 and signed on 2 October 1997 by the foreign ministers of the 15 Member States. It entered into force on 1 May 1999 (the first day of the second month following ratification by the last Member State) after ratification by all the Member States in accordance with their respective constitutional requirements.

From the legal point of view, the Treaty amends certain provisions of the EU Treaty, the treaties establishing the European Communities and certain related acts. It does not replace the other treaties; rather, it stands alongside them.

Troïka

The 'Troïka' consists of the Member State which currently holds the Presidency of the Council, the Member State which held it for the preceding six months and the Member State which will hold it for the next six months. The Troïka is assisted by the Commission and represents the Union in external relations coming under the common foreign and security policy.

The Troïka in its present form has been altered by the Treaty of Amsterdam and replaced by a system whereby the Presidency is assisted by the Secretary-General of the Council, in his capacity as High Representative for the common foreign and security policy, and by the Member State which is next in line for the Presidency.

U

Unanimity

The term 'unanimity' refers to the requirement for all the Member States meeting in the Council to be in agreement before a proposal can be adopted. Since the Single European Act, the unanimity requirement has applied in a much more limited area than before. In the context of the first pillar, voting by qualified majority is now the rule. The second and third pillars, however, still operate exclusively according to the intergovernmental method and the unanimity requirement.

Uniform electoral procedure and composition of the European Parliament

Article 190 of the EC Treaty (former Article 138) requires the European Parliament to draw up proposals for elections by direct universal suffrage under a uniform procedure in all the Member States. This would ensure that the different European political tendencies were more faithfully represented in Parliament. However, all concrete proposals made in the past have foundered on national electoral traditions.

At present the number of seats in Parliament allocated to each country is a compromise between representation according to population and equal representation for all Member States, with the least populous countries being somewhat over-represented. In order to safeguard the effectiveness of Parliament in an enlarged Union, the Treaty of Amsterdam stipulates that the maximum number of members may not exceed 700.

Universal service

Universal service is a concept developed by the Community institutions. It refers to the set of general interest demands to which services such as telecommunications and the mail should be subject throughout the Community. The aim is to ensure that all users have access to quality services at an affordable price.

V

'Variable-geometry' Europe

'Variable-geometry' Europe is the term used to describe the idea of a method of differentiated integration which acknowledges that there are irreconcilable differences within the integration structure and therefore allows for a permanent separation between a group of Member States and a number of less developed integration units.

W

Weighting of votes in the Council

When a decision is taken by qualified majority in the Council, the weighting of votes is the result of a compromise between Member States which, although equal in law, differ in various respects. One factor determining the number of votes a Member State has is the size of its population, with an adjustment which leads to relative over-representation of the countries with a small population.

This system has worked well so far, since it has given legitimacy to the decisions taken. With the current distribution of votes it is impossible for the 'large' countries to combine to put the 'small' countries in a minority and vice versa. This gives a guarantee that decisions taken by qualified majority have the broadest possible support.

With a view to enlargement, a revision of the scale of weightings is being considered to ensure that the relative weight of the 'small' and 'medium-sized' countries is not out of proportion to the size of their population. In addition to this adjustment of the number of votes granted to each Member State, the possible introduction of a 'double majority' system is also being discussed.

Under the Treaty of Amsterdam, a protocol on the institutions has been annexed to the EU Treaty, providing for an intergovernmental conference to be convened at least one year before membership of the Union exceeds 20. Its purpose will be to carry out a comprehensive review of the Treaty provisions on the composition and functioning of the institutions. The Protocol also links the question of the weighting of votes to the number of Commissioners.

A number of Member States and the Commission argue that the weighting of votes and the broader issue of enlargement should be linked to the question of extending qualified majority voting (see the joint declaration by Belgium, France and Italy attached to the Final Act of the Intergovernmental Conference).

Western European Union (WEU)

WEU is an organisation which was set up in 1948 for the purposes of cooperation on defence and security. It consists of 28 countries with four different types of status. Member States, associate members, observers and associate partners. The EU countries have the status of Member State (except Austria, Denmark, Finland, Ireland and Sweden, which have observer status).

The Treaty on European Union raised WEU to the rank of an 'integral part of the development of the Union', while preserving its institutional autonomy, and gave it the task of elaborating and implementing decisions and actions which have defence implications.

WEU associate members

In their Maastricht Declaration of 10 December 1991, the WEU Member States invited the European countries that were members of NATO but not of the European Union to become associate members of WEU. There are six such countries: Iceland, Norway, Turkey and, since March 1999, Hungary, Poland and the Czech Republic. Their associate member status, which was specified in the Petersberg Declaration of 19 June 1992, allows them to participate fully in the meetings of the WEU Council and its working parties. A permanent liaison procedure enables them to be associated with the WEU Planning Cell. They are also entitled to express their views, but cannot veto a decision on which the Member States have reached a consensus. They can associate themselves with their decisions and join in WEU military operations under its command.

WEU associate partners

The status of associated partner was created in 1994 for the 10 central and eastern European countries which have concluded a Europe Agreement with the Union. Since Hungary, Poland, and the Czech Republic became associate members of WEU in 1999, the number of associate partners now stands at seven: Bulgaria, Romania, Slovakia, Slovenia and the three Baltic States. It allows them to attend meetings of the WEU Council, where they are kept regularly informed of the activities of the Council working groups; they may be invited to participate in these groups on an ad hoc basis. They also have a permanent liaison arrangement with the Planning Cell. Finally, they may be involved in decisions taken by the Member States on the tasks listed in the Petersberg Declaration: humanitarian and rescue tasks, peacekeeping tasks, and tasks of combat forces in crisis management including peacemaking.

WEU observers

In their Maastricht Declaration of 10 December 1991 the Member States belonging to WEU proposed that the other EU Member States should be invited to join WEU or to become observers.

Austria, Denmark, Finland, Ireland and Sweden have observer status, which means that they may attend the meetings of the WEU Council, can be invited to meetings of working parties and, on request, may speak at such meetings.

White Paper

Commission White Papers are documents containing proposals for Community action in a specific area. In some cases they follow a Green Paper published to launch a consultation process at European level. Examples include the White Papers on the completion of the internal market, on growth, competitiveness and employment and the approximation of the laws of the associated States of central and eastern Europe in areas of relevance to the internal market. When a White Paper has been favourably received by the Council, it can become the action programme for the Union in the area concerned.

Index

A

B

C

D

E

O

P

European Commission

Glossary
Institutions, policies and enlargement of the European Union

Luxembourg: Office for Official Publications of the European Communities

2000 — 79 pp. — 21 x 29.7 cm

ISBN 92-828-8282-9

European Parliament

Palais de l'Europe
Avenue Robert-Schuman
BP 1024 F
F-67070 Strasbourg Cedex

Plateau du Kirchberg
L-2929 Luxembourg
Rue Wiertz
B-1047 Bruxelles

Internet:
http://www.europarl.eu.int

BELGIQUE/BELGIË

Rue Wiertz/Wiertzstraat
B-1047 Bruxelles/Brussel
Tel. (32-2) 284 20 05
Fax (32-2) 230 75 55
E-mail: epbrussels@europarl.eu.int
Internet:
http://www.europarl.eu.int/brussels

DANMARK

Christian IX's Gade 2, 2.
DK-1111 København K
Tlf. (45) 33 14 33 77
Fax (45) 33 15 08 05
E-post: epkobenhavn@europarl.eu.int
Internet: http://www.europarl.eu.int

DEUTSCHLAND

Europäisches Haus
Unter den Linden 78
D-10117 Berlin
Tel. (49-30) 22 80-1000
Fax (49-30) 22 80-1111
E-Mail: epberlin@europarl.eu.int
Internet: http://www.europarl.eu.int

ΕΛΛΑΔΑ/GREECE

Λεωφόρος Αμαλίας 8
GR-10557 Αθήνα
Τηλ. (30-1) 331 15 41-47
Φαξ: (30-1) 331 15 40
E-mail: epathinai@europarl.eu.int

ESPAÑA

Paseo de la Castellana, 46
E-28046 Madrid
Tel. (34) 914 36 47 47
Fax (34) 915 78 31 71
E-mail: epmadrid@europarl.eu.int
Internet: http://www.europarl.es/euro

Avenida Diagonal, 407 bis
Planta 18
E-08008 Barcelona
Tel. (34) 932 92 01 59
    (34) 93 41 58 77
Fax (34) 932 17 66 82
E-mail: jribot@europarl.eu.int
Internet: http://www.europarl.eu.int

FRANCE

288, boulevard Saint-Germain
F-75341 Paris Cedex 07
Tél. (33) 140 63 40 00
Fax (33) 145 51 52 53
Minitel 3615-3616 Europe
E-mail: epparis@europarl.eu.int
Internet: http://www.europarl.eu.int/paris

2, rue Henri-Barbusse
F-13241 Marseille
Tél. (33) 491 91 46 00
Fax (33) 491 90 09 503
E-mail: isabelle.coustet@france.dg10-bur.cec.be
Internet: http://europarl.eu.int/marseille

1, avenue du Président-Robert-Schuman
BP 1024F
F-67070 Strasbourg Cedex
Tél. (33) 388 17 40 01
Fax (33) 388 17 51 84
E-mail: epstrasbourg@europarl.eu.int

IRELAND

European Union House
43 Molesworth Street
Dublin 2
Ireland
Tel. (353-1) 605 79 00
Fax (353-1) 605 79 99
E-mail: epdublin@europarl.eu.int
Internet: http://www.europarl.eu.int

ITALIA

Via IV Novembre, 149
I-00187 Roma
Tel. (39) 06 69 95 01
Fax (39) 06 69 95 02 00
E-mail: eproma@europarl.eu.int
Internet: http://www.europarl.it

Corso Magenta, 59
I-20123 Milano
Tel. (39) 024 81 86 45
Fax (39) 024 81 46 19
E-mail: mcavenaghi@europarl.eu.int
Internet: http://www.europarl.it

LUXEMBOURG

Bâtiment Robert Schuman
Place de l'Europe
L-2929 Luxembourg
Tél. (352) 43 00-22597
Fax (352) 43 00-22457
E-mail: epluxembourg@europarl.eu.int.
Internet: http://www.europarl.eu.int

NEDERLAND

Korte Vijverberg, 6
2513 AB Den Haag
Nederland
Tel. (31-70) 362 49 41
Fax: (31-70) 364 70 01
E-mail: epdenhaag@europarl.eu.int
Internet: http://www.europarl.eu.int/denhaag

ÖSTERREICH

Kärntnerring 5-7
A-1010 Wien
Tel. (43-1) 51 61 70
Fax (43-1) 513 25 15
E-Mail: epwien@europarl.eu.int
Internet: http://www.europarl.eu.int

PORTUGAL

Largo Jean Monnet, 1-6.°
P-1269-070 Lisboa
Tel.: (351) 213 57 80 31
     (351) 213 57 82 98
Fax: (351) 213 54 00 04
E-mail: eplisboa@europarl.eu.int
Internet: http://www.parleurop.pt

SUOMI/FINLAND

Pohjoisesplanadi 31
FIN-00100 Helsinki
PL 26
FIN-00131 Helsinki
P. (358-9) 622 04 50
F. (358-9) 622 26 10
Sähköposti: ephelsinki@europarl.eu.int
Internet: http://www.europarl.eu.int

Norra esplanaden 31
FIN-00100 Helsingfors
PB 26
FIN-00131 Helsingfors
Tfn (358-9) 622 04 50
Fax (358-9) 622 26 10
E-post: ephelsinki@europarl.eu.int
Internet: http://www.europarl.eu.int

SVERIGE

Nybrogatan 11, 3 tr.
S-114 39 Stockholm
Tfn (46-8) 56 24 44 55
Fax (46-8) 56 24 44 99
E-post: epstocklhom@europarl.eu.int
E-post: info@europarl.se
Internet: http://www.europarl.se

UNITED KINGDOM

2 Queen Anne's Gate
London SW1H 9AA
United Kingdom
Tel. (44-207) 227 43 00
Fax (44-207) 227 43 02
E-mail: eplondon@europarl.eu.int
Internet: http://www.europarl.eu.int/uk

9 Alva Street
Edinburgh EH2 4PH
United Kingdom
Tel. (44-131) 225 20 58
Fax (44-131) 226 41 05
E-mail: wscott@europarl.eu.int
Internet: http://www.europarl.eu.int